Rich On Fifty

How to Start an Investment Club and Build Wealth with Friends for as Little as $50 a Month

By
Chris Kiklas, Jan Johnson, and Jason Smith

Rich on Fifty© 2017 • Rich on Fifty, LLC
All Rights Reserved

Rich on Fifty: How to How to Start an Investment Club and Build Wealth with Friends for as Little as $50 a Month

© 2017 Rich on Fifty

All rights reserved. No part of this publication may be reproduced, distributed, or transmitted in any form or by any means, including photocopying, recording, or other electronic or mechanical methods, without the prior written permission of the publisher, except in the case of brief quotations embodied in critical reviews and certain other noncommercial uses permitted by copyright law.

ISBN 9781521203118

So Why Is This Book Called "Rich on Fifty", Anyway?

This is a book about starting an investment club, and for the most part, investing is intimidating to the vast majority of people—at least it was to us. When we started out, we had no idea what we were doing, and we wanted everyone to be okay with that. We didn't want to make it financially impossible to *get* into the club or have it be a financial burden to *stay* in, month to month, over a period of many years, so we chose $50 as the threshold amount for everyone's monthly investments.

Over time, and much to our surprise, we have amassed quite a bit of money, and we did it *together*, **$50 at a time**. We've seen our money grow in ways we wouldn't have been able to if we just kept sitting on the couch, staying intimidated by all we *didn't* know.

So the moral of the story here is, **JUST START.** $50 at a time may not seem like much in the beginning, but over time you can add to it, and your money will grow, and then one day, you'll look up, and you will, indeed, be "rich on fifty".

Keep up with Rich on Fifty

Facebook: https://www.facebook.com/richonfifty/

Website: https://www.richonfifty.com/

Email: richonfifty@gmail.com

RIGHT UP FRONT, Let Us Say THANK YOU To...

…the AWESOME and AMAZING current members of Stocks & Bondage, without whom the club would not be possible, nor would the wisdom in this book have ever been created.

Bill Baumeyer
Gabrielle Baumeyer
Pam Buck
Shannon Carpenter
Carla Everett
Mattison Grey
Steven Hawkins
Kirk Johnson (ALSO our awesome book cover designer!)
Lucy King
Robin Mack
Jay Mays
Robert Moore
Tamara Siler

Thank you for your time, your attention, your participation, your research, your dedication, your ideas, and for all the questions you asked that made everyone in the club think harder and dig deeper.

Thank you to our beta readers and editors, **Connie Groh, Maureen Hall, Nathan Webb**

Herrington, Ruth Cañas Walker, and **Meredith Ryan.** You made our thoughts clearer, offered great suggestions, and provided awesome early reviews that kept us going!

Thank you to **Eileen Gordon** for supporting, coaching, and encouraging us as well as helping us get the word out about our club and investment successes. Your expertise contributed A LOT, and we are grateful!

Thank you, also, to the members who have come and gone over the years. We hope we made an impression, that you took away some skills, and that somewhere you are out there **right now** getting **RICH ON FIFTY**!

Rich on Fifty
Table of Contents

Welcome Letter xi

Introduction..xiii

Rich on Fifty Manifesto....................................... xxi

Disclaimer..xxii

Chapter 1: Getting Started with an Investment Club 1
   Q: What is an investment club?............................... 1
   Q: Why is an investment club relevant today? Can't you just get all the information that you need online? 2
   Q: So, do I have to start my own investment club, or can I just join one? If I can join one, how do I find them, and how do I know if it's a good club or a good fit for me? 4
   Q: Why did you decide to start—or why did you decide to join—an investment club? 6
   Q: So, why should I do this? Why should I start my own investment club? 8
   Q: How did you go about getting this thing off the ground? 12
   Q: Why do you want to help other people create and manage their own investment clubs? 16

Chapter 2: The People or Members................... 21
   Q: How does it work having multiple people investing in one place? 21
   Q: Who Owns What and How Much?.................... 22

Q: Who are the right people to be in the club? 24
Q: How do you deselect Members for the club? How do you kick people out? 30
Q: Am I going to want to hang out with these people? 31
Q: Is this the only place that club Members invest? 33

Chapter 3: Knowledge and Experience 39
Q: Do your Members have a lot of investment experience? 39
Q: Can you do this when you don't know anything? What if I don't know anything? 41
Q: Prior to joining the club, what other investment experiences have you had? 44
Q: How would you rate your investment knowledge now that you've been in the club for several years? 50

Chapter 4: Operations 57
Q: What are the legal things that we have to do to start an investment club? 57
Q: What else do we have to do, legally? 58
Q: What kinds of records should our club be keeping? 60
Q: Who's in charge and how did you decide that? 62
Q: What are the biggest challenges the club faces when putting together an agenda? 68
Q: So, what about the tax implications of this? Are there any? 71

Chapter 5: Running a Meeting 77
Preparation 77
Suggested Agenda Format 78

Chapter 6: Money and Cost 85

Q: What are the typical club expenses that you could expect? 85
Q: How do you decide to pay those expenses? Who pays them? 86
Q: Can I afford this? 87
Q: Is the money that I put into this club mine? Whose money is this? 89
Q: So, how rich can I get here? 91
Q: What kind of returns should somebody in an investment club look forward to? 93
Look at you! You're halfway through the book! GOOD JOB! 97

Chapter 7: Risk 99
Q: How trustworthy are these people in the investment club? Can they or will they steal my money? 99
Q: How risky is this, really? 101
Q: Is this going to work? 103

Chapter 8: Strategy 107
Q: Does the club have an investment strategy or philosophy? 107
Q: Does your club's investment strategy match your personal investment strategy? 110

Chapter 9: Stock Picking 113
Q: What kinds of investments does your club make and why? 113
Q: How do you decide what you buy? What do you look for in a stock? 115
Q: As an investment club Member, what is it exactly that we're investing in? What am I getting for my $50? 117
Q: So, how does one pick a stock? 118
Q: How do you know when to sell and what to sell? 120

Q: What if we pick the wrong stock?....................125

Chapter 10: Teaching and Learning.................129
Q: So, who's going to teach me in this investment club?..129
Q: What are some of the best resources that you have found while starting your club? 131
Q: What are some of the worst resources you found when starting your club?.............................132
Q: What investment concepts seem to be the most difficult for people to grasp? 138

Chapter 11: Participation 143
Q: What kind of time commitment is this going to take? How much time? 143
Q: How do you encourage club Members to remain involved?...148
Q: How do you make investing interesting for people who are not at all interested in investing? 150

Chapter 12: The Impact 153
Q: How has being involved in an investment club changed your own investing activities?...............153
Q: How has the club changed over the years?..158

Chapter 13: Hindsight..163
Q: What's the one thing that you wish you had done when setting up the club that you did not do? 163
Q: If you had to do it all over again, what would you have done differently? 168

Chapter 14: Reflection...171
Q: What are some of your major investing successes? 171
Q: What are some of your worst picks? 174

Q: What's been the biggest obstacle to starting and/or running an investment club?...................... 177
Q: What's the most important or surprising thing that you have learned so far? 180
Q: What are three concrete pieces of advice that you would give to people who are thinking about starting an investment club of their own?............ 183

Chapter 15: The Future....................................... 187
Q: Here it is. Here's the ultimate finishing question. Where would you like to see your own club be in the next five years? 187

Conclusion.. 191

Your Club's First Year 193

About the Authors 199
WOWZA! You've FINISHED the book! 201

x

Welcome Letter

May 4, 2017

Hey, you gorgeous, brilliant reader you!

Yeah, we're talking to you, beautiful.

When we started the Stocks and Bondage investment club back in 2008, we were probably right where you are today. We had this broad idea of what an investment club was, we knew some people who had been in one before, and we still had no idea how to start one or if it would be worth it in the end.

So we bought books. Lots of books. And at the end of the day, we still had no idea. It took us awhile to figure out if this was something we really wanted to do and even longer to really get a grasp on how to do it.

Yeah, even after all those books.

And that's why we are here today. In our 9th year of operation, Stocks and Bondage is still going strong, still making money, and still learning. Just for kicks, we went back out to see if there were any good resources on starting an investment club, and we were amazed to see...well, the same books that were there 9 years prior that left us fending for ourselves.

Knowing that, we could not just stand idly by, so we decided to start Rich on Fifty. Rich on Fifty is a collection of resources to help you figure out if this is right for you (that's what this book is designed to do), hold your hand while you start your own club (which we do through the courses on our website, richonfifty.com), connect you with other investment clubs around the world (at our online forums), and help you learn how to make money with your club.

With that being said, curl up next to that fireplace with a glass of merlot, and let's get this party started!

Chris, Jan, and Jason

Introduction

Jantroductions

Let me introduce you to Jason Smith and Chris Kiklas[1], two partners in our investment club, Stocks & Bondage, and in this broader project that grew from there, *Rich on Fifty.*

Jason is one of the calmest, most thoughtful people on the planet, and I knew back in 2008 that I wanted him to be in the investment club I was putting together—I just didn't know then what an awesome contribution he would turn out to be. I often joke that Jason is the "No" in our club, but what I really mean is that he doesn't just go along because everyone else is saying "Yes" to something. He thinks things through, he doesn't rush to judgment, and he isn't afraid to go against the flow. Sure, we outvote him every now and then, but he's the one person I look to when a decision seems to be "too easy" or "a no-brainer." I actually *seek out* his brain instead. He's quiet where I am loud, he

---

[1] I met Chris and Jason both through **Landmark Worldwide**. If you don't already know about the work of this transformational company, you should look them up and then just go REGISTER for the first course they offer at the next possible available date in whatever city you can get to. Trust me when I say ***the Landmark Forum will forever change your life***.

always has a fresh perspective on a company or its stock, and he thinks of things that never even occurred to me--all of which I value highly. It also helps that Jason is a Quality Engineer, which (to me) means he's logical, analytical, and focused on improvements. If that's not reason enough right there to have him in an investment club, I don't know what is.

You want someone like Jason in your club to balance out all the impulsive folks (like me), and you want someone like him to be your friend because he's going to keep his cool while everyone else around you (including you) is melting down.

Chris is my partner in crime—any crime. Whatever I'm up to, he's game to try. Whatever idea I have, I can bounce it off him, and he will help me run with it. He has started companies, launched products, led people, and coached teams. We have volunteered together and served on a local nonprofit board, and he never fails to impress me with his creativity and his dedication to whatever task is before him. His brain is a constant source of ideas, amusements, diversions, and projects, and I know that no matter what craziness I can dream up, he will take it to the next level and re-inspire me right back.

It's Chris who deserves the credit for the book

you are holding in your hands. What started out as a nice idea on a random Sunday quickly morphed under his leadership into a series of structures, chapters, courses, and plans designed to make investment clubs cool, and it's all because of him—even the Rich on Fifty name! He's passionate about technology and has used every productivity app ever developed, which comes in handy when I need to get off my butt and get into action.

So now you know a little bit about both of these amazing men, and you'll learn more when you hear from them in their own words throughout this book. I hope you can hear our individual voices inside our collective efforts, and I encourage you to get in touch with us directly to learn more and contribute to *our* education in the process.

Now, let's get RICH!

Christroductions

In case you haven't figured out what's going on, we are each going to introduce each other to you. It's not that we like to talk about each other and lavish praise on ourselves but to show you how different people can have a different view on other people. When we get to the chapter about who to let in your group, remember this introduction. Look at everyone you know from different angles, ask them different questions, and really get to know them from all sides.

Jason is one of the first people I met at the initial Stocks & Bondage meeting, and I distinctly remember thinking I was totally in the wrong club. This was a group of people that Jan put together, and the only person in that group I knew was Jan. And even Jan I did not know well. I had no clue what I was getting into, I felt incredibly uncomfortable surrounded by all these strangers that had no problems being incredibly social with each other, and I just wanted to go home.

And then I shook Jason's hand, he said hello, introduced himself, and was so confident in his demeanor and personality that I suddenly felt like I was in the right place. That's the kind of power that Jason has in a room—crazy, confident love for everyone.

Over the next few months, when this raucous group of strangers was trying to find their way and coming up with outlandish ideas of what an investment club should be, Jason was the one voice that I knew I could always count on to help direct the conversation back to sanity, who always made sure that, no matter how far off the trail we wandered, that we always found our way back to camp.

What you can always expect from Jason throughout the work of Rich on Fifty is for details and well thought out ideas. Where Jan and I come up with what may seem like completely unconnected thoughts and ideas, Jason is the one who will step you through how it all actually, in the end, makes sense.

Jan was leading a seminar in 2008 on living outside the box and being the cause of breakthroughs in your own life[2]. There are pieces of advice from that seminar that have fundamentally shaped the way I work and help me accomplish everything I want to accomplish[3]. For example, Jan said, "Everyone, every week is at risk of having something go wrong, some kind of breakdown in their lives, at their work. So why not plan for it? I schedule my breakdowns ahead of time. On my calendar every Friday afternoon, I schedule four hours for them. Then when a breakdown *does* happen in the middle of the week, I can shift whatever they interrupted over to Friday afternoon. And then on the weeks where there are no breakdowns? Then I have four hours to do whatever the hell I want."

---

[2] See Jan's previous footnote about Landmark Worldwide. I can't say enough positive things about what I've received from attending Landmark courses.

[3] For what it's worth, also the things I *thought* were important, what ended up not being important and knowing when to cut those things from my life.

I am an idea guy; it's what I thrive on. Many days, I am not totally present to what is going on around me because I am always stuck there, thinking about things. Jan is one of those people who can pierce through that veil of thought and help me weigh my thoughts, my dreams, my ambitions and everything else that is going on in my life, so that I can be more focused and more driven and really achieve what I want to achieve.

She is also that person that, when I am stuck, will tell me like it is, even when it hurts. She sees me for who I really am and for the man I can be. She is my cheerleader, my coach, my confidante, and my therapist.

What you can rely on her for in this program is to also be your cheerleader. She has the passion and the drive to see you succeed. She wants to be there for all of you, help you create a new community of investors, and change the way the world looks at finances.

I am confident that with the support of the three of us and your own amazing ability and thirst for knowledge, you will have an incredible journey into creating your own investment club!

Jasintroductions

If **Jan** isn't the craziest person I know, she's up at the top. I definitely mean that in a positive way. If there is something she wants done, nothing will stop her from getting it done. She doesn't care if the bank tells her no, she doesn't care if the school tells her no, she doesn't care if it is currently "not possible". She will find a way to get it done.

Jan is also one of the most productive people I know. Running a very successful educational grant writing and consulting company, owning multiple Airbnb locations, participating fully in life, and starting richonfifty.com with us wasn't enough; she added licensed real estate agent to her accomplishments last year.

Jan's invitation to the investment club got me to come to the first meeting and her energy, drive, and passion has been invaluable to the club. I feel privileged that I can count Jan as one of my friends and business partners and enjoy her company whenever we are together.

I met **Chris** through participation in the investment club. From the start, it was obvious that Chris was someone who could be a trusted leader. If thoughtful intensity is a thing, Chris has it. If it's not a thing, he invented it.

Chris combines creativity and structure very successfully. He can creatively come up with solutions to problems and new ideas in one moment and then keep us structured with an agenda and timeline in the next moment. I definitely appreciate his ability to keep us all on track.

I don't think my brief introduction does justice to each of these fabulous people. They are remarkable, fabulous, productive, and successful in life and I love having each of them in my life.

Now let's get busy getting this investment club started!

Rich on Fifty Manifesto

We did this, and you can do this, too. We are here to show you how to start and how to succeed.

Investing can be complex, but it needn't be overly complicated. Real humans do it all the time. It *can* be figured out, and we will help you.

This is a community of learning, and we learn together. We will teach you what we know, but you are also responsible for taking what you learn from us, adding what you already know, putting it all into action, expanding on it, and teaching others.

You learn best by doing, not just reading. So read, discuss, do, then read, discuss, and do some more.

You don't have to get it right, you just have to get it going. Start the conversation, start your club, and start investing for yourself and your future.

Disclaimer

Be advised that investments may go up as well as down for any reason, and past performance of a stock is no guarantee of future performance.

Rich on Fifty makes no representation as to the timeliness, accuracy, or suitability of any content in this book and website, and its authors cannot be held liable for any irregularity or inaccuracy.

Stock recommendations and comments in this book and website are solely opinions of analysts and experts quoted or those of the Rich on Fifty staff. They do not represent the opinions of Rich on Fifty on whether to buy, sell, or hold shares of any particular stock.

All readers and investors are advised to conduct their own independent research before making an investment decision. Investors should consider the source and suitability of any investment advice for their needs. Your use of this book, website, and their contents, is at your own risk.

Links from this book or website to third-party websites are in no way an endorsement by Rich on Fifty of their content or their suitability for any purpose.

Chapter 1: Getting Started with an Investment Club

CHRIS: This is Chris.

JASON: This is Jason.

JAN: And this is Jan.

CHRIS: And we're going to kick this off by covering the very basics of an investment club. Let's start with the most obvious question.

Q: What is an investment club?

JAN: An investment club is a group of people who come together to learn about investing and they do this by pooling their money so they can collectively make investments that are bigger than they could make themselves. At Rich on Fifty, we believe an investment club is a learning laboratory, and as our Manifesto states, we see the $50 a month each Member invests as tuition for the learning we do together. I think that's the biggest benefit of an investment club.

CHRIS: Some people may already know what they're doing and they just want to get together with a larger group of people so that they can invest larger sums of money. But with this book, we're really targeting the people who don't have a lot of information or knowledge about investing but want to learn.

Q: Why is an investment club relevant today? Can't you just get all the information that you need online?

CHRIS: It's even more relevant today because we are inundated with so much information online that one human being who is not used to learning about investing is going to be completely lost and confused by just going through that one channel. You might find 80 different websites explaining revenue a different way, but until you talk it out with a group of people, you may never really understand it.

JAN: I think you get information fatigue, too. After a certain point, there's so much information out there that you just give up or you just say, "Well, I can't possibly understand this because there are too many resources." What we're doing with Rich on Fifty is culling that information, giving people like you the bare minimum of what you need, plus just a little bit extra—enough to whet your appetite and point you in the right direction. From here, you can do more research on your own if you'd like, but at least we've narrowed the field and gotten you started.

JASON: Yes, you probably *can* get all the information you need online. When people do research on an individual stock or investing topic, most of their stuff is going to come from online resources. But one of the benefits you're not going to get by yourself is the different points of view from your fellow investment club Members. For example, I rarely go to Starbucks (SBUX), but we have people in our club who love Starbucks and go there a lot. In fact, one of our Members was a manager there for a long time. So if we're talking about Starbucks' operations, how people perceive the company, or their customer satisfaction, other people's experiences and perceptions can make a big difference in the club's decision to buy the stock or not.

CHRIS: Another thing is that it doesn't matter the strength of your Google Kung Fu; there's still a chance that you're going to get some information that isn't accurate or that you'll need to know a lot more in order to make a good decision. How many times in our club have people brought up wanting to invest in some penny stock[4] that they saw and they thought that that was a great deal because somebody told them, "You could buy 8,000 of these for really cheap, and it's going to go up 8,000% in the next six months," and they really believed that that was the case, and it wasn't until they came back to the investment club that we all talked through it and they figured out that that was just a scam. Having the balance of other people's experience and perspectives is a major contribution to your investment knowledge.

Q: So, do I have to start my own investment club, or can I just join one? If I can join one, how do I find them, and how do I know if it's a good club or a good fit for me?

JASON: Well, you can definitely join one, but Rich on Fifty is going to show you *how* to start an investment club, and it's just as simple as getting your friends together, or friends of your

---

[4] Penny stocks are common shares of small public companies that trade at low prices per share. The Securities and Exchange Commission defines a penny stock as a security (a tradable financial asset such as a stock or bond) that trades below $5 per share, is not listed on a national exchange, and fails to meet other specific criteria. Stocks & Bondage does not invest in penny stocks, though some Members may do so in their personal portfolios.

friends, and all of you learning together.

CHRIS: I'm a longtime fan of gaming, and in huge online games, you'll see people running around with "LFG" bubbles over their heads (looking for group), so I guess in the real world you could wear a button around that says, "Looking for an investment club," and you could wait until somebody walks up to you and says, "Hey, I've got one!" Probably not super practical. But if you're starting your own, then you'll know the people you're getting involved with—at least to some degree. If you are just looking to join one, it's going to take a lot more effort to figure out if you're a good fit or not. That's not what we're about. We're about helping you to start an investment club of your own.

JAN: Before I started this club, I actually went to a meeting of another club, and I did not like the vibe. During the meeting I attended, they proposed a stock that was very confusing to me, and I think it was confusing to them. I just didn't understand why they were interested in buying it. Granted, I was only there for one meeting, but I was invited to join their club, and I declined. I think it's harder to find a fit than it is to create the fit, which is why I started my own club.

Q: Why did you decide to start— or why did you decide to join—an investment club?

JAN: In 2008, when everyone was saying "the economy was going to hell," I thought, "There's got to be an opportunity here to make some money because not everything is going to go down at the same time in the same way." I have this sign in my office that says, "Opportunities exist in all market cycles," and so I wondered, "What would be the opportunity right now—in THIS cycle?"

I had been wanting to invest in stocks for quite a while, and I knew I should start investing my money *now* as opposed to just hoping that wherever I had put my money years ago was going to do well in the future. But I also knew I needed the structure of other people and the accountability. So, when I decided to start the club, my thought process was, "Okay, I'm interested. I don't know enough on my own, but I know a little bit, and I certainly know enough cool, smart people who would also be interested. If I could just put them all together in the same room, we could probably really have something here."

JASON: A lot of Jan's remarks speak to me as well. I wanted to know more about investing. I wanted to understand all the stuff I saw and read about a stock, like how do I analyze that stock, and how can I make money off of this? That's really why I joined—for the education and the company of people we got together. I knew I could say, "I wouldn't mind hanging out with these people—at least for now."

CHRIS: I had three reasons why I wanted to join an investment club.

The first is I just had some personal investing experience that was pretty terrible before I joined the club, and I really wanted to learn more. When Jan was pitching this to her friends, she talked about the importance of gaining knowledge and understanding and learning how to invest.

The second reason was my mom was getting close to retirement age and, as we started talking about what she needed to do before retirement, we really found out that she didn't even know where all of her own retirement money was. She didn't know how much money she had saved up for retirement. She didn't know the investments she had—if they were stocks, if they were bonds, if they were doing well, if they weren't doing well—and we looked through that and finally realized she was going to be okay. As a result of that, I started looking at my own portfolio and realized that I didn't have the retirement pension fund that she was going to have and that I really need to pay a lot more attention to that; otherwise, when I got to be her age, I was going to be a lot worse off than she is.

The third reason I wanted to join was for the social aspect of it. For at least one day a month, I knew that I was going to get out of the house and that I was going to be with a group of people that I don't often see. To me, it was kind of a neat social opportunity as well.

JAN: Yeah, that's an important part, too. I'm definitely here for the knowledge, but the social part is really interesting, and I never miss a meeting unless I am out of town, and I try to arrange my schedule around that because it's valuable to me on all those different levels.

Q: So, why should I do this? Why should I start my own investment club?

CHRIS: You should do this because every day you should be learning something new. When you join an investment club and you actively participate, you're going to be stretching your mind, and you're going to be learning something new every day and in unexpected ways! The more you are involved—the more you learn about the business world and about stocks and bonds and investing and the terminology and how things run—the more global conversations you can actually take part in.

Since joining the club, I've subscribed to *The Wall Street Journal* and *The New York Times*. I've subscribed to *Fast Company*. I read finance blogs all the time. I read about businesses all the time. It has totally reshaped what I do in my spare time, and I've gotten really excited about it. I think that's why you should do it—because you really learn and change and adapt in a whole different way than you would have otherwise.

JASON: The group aspect is key. What's really beneficial is that you're not doing all that learning on your own. You could spend your time finding out about this company or that company, but the fact is that other people are doing that research for you. They're also bringing in the knowledge; you're not just off in a class somewhere or learning about stocks on your own. Plus, it gives you confidence. Maybe buying stocks is a little scary the first time. You may think, "I don't know what I'm doing. How do I pick the right stock?" So, you start an investment club where your entry fee is not all that much—$50 a month—and you get ten people together. You can then buy $500 worth of stock at a time and then, after a year, you're like, "We made some money! We can actually do this thing! Wow! Maybe I can do this on my own as well," and you can continue to build that confidence level and build your personal portfolio.

CHRIS: And there are stocks that, if you were only investing $50 a month on your own, you would never be able to buy. Even, as a club, investing $500 a month can sometimes mean only buying one share of something. But that is one share you may not ever have been able to buy on your own.

The more success we see in this club, the more confident I become on my own, and not just about investing but also in talking about money. The conversation of money is a tough conversation to have, and the more often you have that conversation, the more comfortable you feel with it and the more power you develop over what you think.

JAN: You should do this because it's not that hard. Yes, the world of investing can be very complex and complicated, and there are pork belly futures and derivative swaps and whatever other craziness there is in the financial world, but starting and running an investment club does not have to be hard. People buy and sell stocks every single day — normal people, regular people, people with more (and certainly less) knowledge than we have — and it's not that difficult. I think doing it and getting over the hump of that initial fear teaches you that it's not that hard and, you know, you're a grown-up and you should pay attention to this.

The other reason, too—and maybe this is really an answer to why do I like the club—is that it makes me pay more attention to things in the world. Yes, the stock might be doing X or Y or Z, but I just paid attention to two news articles about a new product that's coming out or I read about a scientific breakthrough in something, and that makes me interested, which sends me down an investing research tunnel. And so it just connects me more to what's going on in the world. I also totally agree that this makes me feel more confident as well.

CHRIS: I love the feeling that it makes me feel more connected to the world, and not just to the United States because, when you start investing in stocks, you start reading up on these companies, and you find out that it's not just US companies that are on the US stock exchanges. That's what we focus on—the US stock exchange—but we've invested in Chinese stocks as well. We've also looked at stocks from other countries. And so you have to learn what's going on in those countries, and it really makes you feel like you're playing more on the global level.

Q: How did you go about getting this thing off the ground?

JAN: Well, at the most basic level, I sent an email to about forty people and I just laid it out there and said, "Here's an opportunity. I have a little bit of investing information. I don't have a whole lot, but I want to have more. I'm interested, are you interested? We're going to learn together. It doesn't matter if you know a lot or you don't. We'll figure this out together. All you have to do is be interested. If you're interested, show up on this day."

We got about fifteen or so people who were interested enough at the beginning to come together in my living room. Some of those people ended up being our founding Members and they're still here. Some of those people joined, but they didn't stay very long and they left. That's all fine. But how we got off the ground is we just sent out an email and invited people. I like to think it was a pretty enrolling email. [And we'll even help you get started with that![5]]

But you can't just say, "Be in my club." You've got to give people a reason and speak to their interests. We met at my house on a Sunday

---

[5] https://www.richonfifty.com/resources/

afternoon, and we just talked about ourselves—about what our fears were and what we were good at and what we weren't good at and how we might go about doing this, and we kind of pieced it together ourselves after that. Remember, we didn't have this book that you have now!

We did look at some resources in a really boring book on starting an investment club. After a few pages, we agreed to just throw it out. Instead of trying to follow someone else's dry instructions, we decided to create the club that we wanted. We stumbled through all of that so you don't have to.

CHRIS: I think we also had tacos.

JAN: Did we?

CHRIS: I'm pretty sure we had tacos.

JAN: There was probably food, you're right!

CHRIS: I think there were tacos, and that's why I went.

It was more than just that first meeting. That first meeting was really just a general interest meeting and we weeded a lot of people out at that meeting, but it took us about four months to weed everybody out who was not totally interested. Like Jan said, a lot of us went online and scoured the internet for information. We bought books (boring books). We subscribed to newsletters (which confused me more than the books). We did all kinds of stuff. But I'll tell you that there's not one of them that I read cover to cover — not a single one.

JAN: Yeah. Not a single one.

CHRIS: And that's why we're doing this — because we created the club that we wanted to create and now we're here to give you the tools to help you create the club that *you* want to create.

JAN: And to demystify it for you so that you don't feel like you have to read that boring investment book or that you have to have the same investment philosophy that we do or that somebody else does or that you have to have a "balanced portfolio"[6] with stocks and bonds and this and that. Maybe you want that; maybe you don't want that. The idea is to make the club that *you* want and to put together something that resonates with *you* and that gets *you* excited about it. Like so many things in life you want to

---

[6] What constitutes a "balanced portfolio" depends on who you ask, how old you are, and how much risk (or uncertainty), you can tolerate. But everyone is different, and what your personal portfolio should contain is something you should decide on your own - later. Don't worry about it now. For now, JUST GET STARTED.

do, you just have to find your entry point.

For a lot of people, this investment club was their entry point into investing, and they've gone on to do bigger things from there.

JASON: Jan said, "I just sent out this email," but I got clear that Jan is a driver, and I am not a driver. You may be reading this and thinking, "Well, I don't know that I'm a driver. Could I drive this? Could this be my club, and could I be running it?" I'm really analytical. I could go in there and I could analyze all this stuff, I'd do the math, I'd do the spreadsheets.

The simple fact is any one of us could have sent out that email to forty people that we know, and you can do it, too. The right people will get together. You've just got to know that they will. You're going to want people who are drivers—people who will take on leadership from the start--and you want some people who will be more analytical, who can help out with the math. But any one of you reading right now can start this and get it off the ground. Don't think, "Oh, I'm going to have to be the president if I start this." Jan hasn't...have you ever been the president?

JAN: I have not, no.

JASON: Never been the president. And she was

the one who did initially send out the email.

CHRIS: The fire-starter.

JASON: Or you can be sitting there, thinking, "Yeah, I'm going to be the president. What are you talking about, Jason? You're crazy!" Or you can be sitting there, thinking, "Whoa! Can I do this? I don't want to be the president." Yes, you can do this.

Q: Why do you want to help other people create and manage their own investment clubs?

JAN: I want to demystify things for people because even the word "investment" sounds kind of grown-up and snooty and arrogant and it can be really high-minded, but I mean, we invest our time, we invest our energy, we invest our resources—whatever they are—in all kinds of things every day of our lives. Money is just another place to invest. I don't know about you, but I'm planning on retiring one day, and I'm going to need some money that's been working for me, so I want to invest for myself, and I want to help other people know that they can do that, too.

CHRIS: Outside of Rich on Fifty, my job is helping businesses become more efficient.

That's what I do. It's what I'm known for—simplifying processes, making things run better, making things easier for people to do. And I was so frustrated when we were starting this club! It took us over a year before we actually got really up and rolling and moving with a process and got everything right just because we didn't know what we were doing when we started out.

I can just imagine that there are thousands of people in this country who would love to do something like this. They take fifteen or twenty minutes to look online. They read one of those other books and then they go, "Forget it. I'm just going to do it." I don't want you to have that "forget it" moment with us. I want you to be able to go through this step-by-step and say, "Ah, I can do this. This is easy."

JASON: Yes, because it was. It was a good year, and we've made some really good returns on our money. We'll talk more about that. But if we could have cut a year off of that time by buying what we're giving out to you right now…

JAN: We would have.

JASON: It would have been phenomenal.

CHRIS: Yeah, absolutely.

JASON: Yeah.

Things to Remember

- An investment club is a group of likeminded people who pool their ideas and their money to invest together. At Rich on Fifty, we are going to help you get a stock-focused investment club up and running.
- While you can get tons of information on investing online, it is oftentimes scary if you are starting from the very beginning. Learning and investing with people you know and trust can help build your confidence to do more investing on your own.
- People start or join investment clubs for lots of different reasons, and that is totally ok.

Homework

- Yes, really, there is homework. Do you have to do it? No, of course not. You are a grown-ass person, and you can do what you want, but if you DO take on the homework, you will be much better prepared for getting your investment club from idea to reality. None of this should take long, and it is all easy to do. And if you need help, we are here for you every step of the way.

- Why do *you* want to start an investment club? Get a notebook and write this down so you can refer to it later. Later, you can also ask your club Members to share why *they* want to be *in* an investment club. You may be surprised by the variety of answers you get.
- What kind of role do you want to take in the investment club? Really think about this one. Are you the leader or the firestarter or both? The answer could be "neither", too, but it is important to know sooner rather than later what kind of contribution you want to make to the club during the startup days.
- Start making a list of people you know. Friends, family, co-workers, people you see at yoga, neighbors—really anyone. Don't edit this list just yet, just write it down. Don't worry, you aren't going to be sending out invitations to everyone just yet. For now, just write the list.

Chapter 2: The People or Members

At this point, you've read Chapter 1, and you've done the (very easy) homework, right? You know why you want to start your own investment club, you've thought about what role you want to play, and you have a list of potential Members. GOOD JOB! So now let's talk about getting all these people together and what happens next.

Q: How does it work having multiple people investing in one place?

CHRIS: The mechanics of the club are pretty simple. Everyone contributes the same amount of money[7].

---

[7] There can be some exceptions. Don't freak out about this. For example, in our club, we use the last two cents of each deposit to indicate who made the deposit to make it easier for the treasurer. It's just a couple cents different for each person. Ex: Jan invests $50.01, Chris invests $50.02, Jason invests $50.03, etc. Also, we allow for Members to add in more than $50 a month. This is something that comes up when you are working on your club's bylaws.

In our club, each Member invests $50 a month, so if your club also chooses to have each Member invest $50 per month, and you have ten Members, at the end of the month you've got $500 that you can invest, which means that you can buy more expensive stocks or just more shares of them. If you were only going to invest that $50 by yourself, you would be limited to stocks that were $50 or less per share. But if you have $500, you can buy stocks that are $100, $200 — anything up to $500 per share. You can also buy multiple shares, not just one, and since you have to pay a fee, in most cases, for every transaction you make[8], it is actually a better return on your investment for that.

Q: Who Owns What and How Much?

Each active Member owns a percent of the club, and the club owns a **portfolio** of stocks. How many stocks and how much the club owns (the club assets) is based on the amount of money that the Members have put into the club over time.

---

[8] There are bare-bones apps such as Robinhood that allow you to make trades for free. Our club uses E*TRADE, which (as of March 2017) charges a $6.95 transaction fee to buy or sell each stock. The E*TRADE platform provides a wealth of online tools and stock research that we use to help us decide what to buy. You might choose another platform, such as Merrill Edge, Schwab, or TD Ameritrade. There are also others.

For example:

Let's say our club, Stocks & Bondage (more about naming your club later!), has a total of $60,000 invested in various stocks. Depending on how long each person has been in the club, they own different percentages of the club's total portfolio. Jan, Jason, and Chris have been in the club since the beginning (2009), so we three each own roughly the same percent of the club's total portfolio. By contrast, a Member who joined our club six months ago owns a much smaller percent of the portfolio.

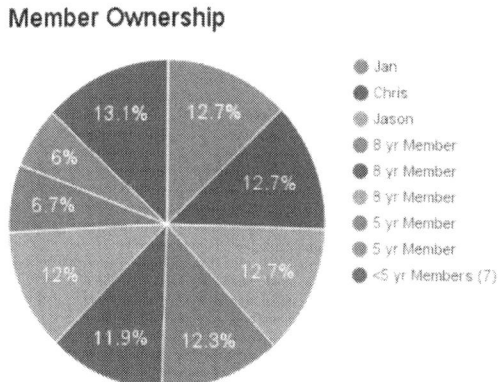

JAN: Simply put, we all pool our money each month, and by majority vote, we decide what stocks we are going to buy. At the most basic level, that is how it works.

Q: Who are the right people to be in the club?

CHRIS: The smart and pretty ones.

JAN: That would be us.

JASON: That *would* be us!

CHRIS: But, since we can't be in every club…

JAN: We can though, virtually, through Rich on Fifty. We *can be* in every club!

Seriously, though, the "right people" in the club are the people who are interested. The right people in the club are the people you want to hang out with. Let me qualify that. There are people who want to be in the club that I don't think are the right people for our club — for whatever reason. Maybe I don't think they're going to participate strongly or consistently. Maybe I think they're going to need too much hand-holding or they're going to want us to do all their thinking for them. I am looking for people who bring something to the table.

Now, granted, when we started, I didn't have that mindset. I just thought, "I want people who are interested." I naively assumed that everybody would participate equally, and that is not the case. But people participate in different ways. If you're in our club and you are still here nine years later, you're the right person on some level because you're at least interested *enough*; you're committed, you've been here, you show up month after month, and by now you are certainly participating because we don't let you *not* participate.

For me, the right people are those for whom I can answer YES when I ask myself, "Are they interested? Will they participate? And do I want to hang out with them?"

CHRIS: That's a great way to categorize it.

JASON: Also, one way of looking at it is the people who show up, they're the right people for the club.

JAN: Exactly, and I wouldn't have invited those forty people if I didn't think I could answer "Yes" to those three questions for each one of them. To get that list of forty people, I went through over 400 people in my contacts, and there were many people who were *not* invited, I can assure you.

Also, in my conversation with people in general, sometimes if the topic of investing comes up, I will say, "Well, I have an investment club and we're doing this and this." I don't say it to put it in front of people or to brag in any way. It's just normal conversation. People who are interested will say, "Oh, you have an investment club? Tell me about that." And so those are also the right people—the people that are attracted to your program. Attraction, not promotion, as they say, and we've gotten a couple of Members that way also. They see me post things on our **Rich on Fifty Facebook page**[9], or they've heard me talk about it because I'm excited about what we're doing. It's cool. We're doing cool stuff! When people have heard me talk about it several times, after a while, they'll say, "I'm interested in that. Are you accepting new Members?" Depending on if we are or not, I'll let them know, but that's another way to find the right people—talk about what you're doing, see who shows up.

JASON: What if I don't know who I should *not* invite? What if I don't know anything about this?

JAN: Well, then start by asking yourself who do you want to hang out with? Who do you think is smart in some way? They've got to bring some smarts to the table. When I invited you, Jason, I didn't really know that you were analytical. I just knew you were smart, and I knew you had a quiet thoughtfulness about you. Where I'm loud and quick to decide, I knew that

---

[9] https://www.facebook.com/richonfifty/

you had a more thoughtful approach, and I wanted you to be part of the club because that was something that I didn't have. But it wasn't just because, "Oh, I think he's cute" or "Oh, I'm friends with him" or "He sits next to my cubicle at work." I mean, those are not good enough reasons, but somebody who can bring something to the table, especially something that I don't have, that is who I want.

CHRIS: I think there are also those friends — and we all have them — that say "No" to everything. You know, those people who, if you're having a party and you said, "Would you like to come?" if they're a 50-percenter, then 50% of the time, they're going to say "Yes," and 50% of the time, they say "No," and of the times they say "Yes," they end up not going — most of the time, anyway. That's not something you want in your club.

You want somebody who you know has the integrity to keep up with it, actually attend the meetings — someone who's really going to participate, and that you get along with. Jan, you said something that was really key there, too. You said that you went through your contact list. That's a great place to start because those are people that you should already get along with. You're going to skip the people who are trolling you or who are just trying to keep up with their exes on Facebook. Don't call those people. Call the people who you really know and respect on social media.

JASON: Yeah, and I like what Jan said about me being smart.

JAN: It's true, though! I mean, you know, everybody has some unique perspective, and it's interesting because several of the people who are in that smart, thoughtful, reflective category brought something to the table but didn't end up staying with us. They left for whatever reason, and that's fine.

One friend left because he wanted to go back to school and he didn't have the energy and the time to give to the club, and he wanted to spend his money on something else, but he is very thoughtful, and we might even extend an invitation to him to come back now that he's working and out of school.

Some of the people who you think will stick with it don't, and some of the people who you think won't, do because they want to learn. It's interesting, but at least start out with that perspective of, "Do I want to hang out with you, and are you smart enough to be my friend?"

JASON: You can invite any person or group that you want. I think it's good if you have someone who's willing to drive things, someone who's willing to follow the rules in terms of "Hey, we need to vote on this," someone who's smart enough to sign up for an E*TRADE account and figure out how to use it. If you're interested in learning and you get other people who are interested in learning—and not just learning the easy way, I mean actually getting your hands dirty, figuring stuff out, sharing it with people, talking about it, being wrong, being right, learning new things—those are the people who are going to be the right people.

JAN: I would also like to point out—and this is specific to our club but I didn't intend it to be this way—is that the majority of the people in our club are all connected through Landmark. The transformational work of Landmark, just the foundation of it, is that people have straight conversations and they have integrity—or at least strive for that—and they do what they say they're going to do.

And, yes, we're all human and we have failings and nobody's perfect, but that common ground of conversation which is, "We want to create something that is bigger than ourselves" was important also. And not everybody in our club now has that same connection; we've got several people that didn't come to us through that channel, but that was another gelling factor for us.

Q: How do you deselect Members for the club? How do you kick people out?

CHRIS: We've never actually evicted anybody from the Stocks & Bondage house before. But we also had a rough time figuring out how we were going to sell stocks, so we just have a hard time letting go, I think.

What we have done—because we have had people leave the club—is we just have a really straight conversation with people who are not participating or if their goals for the club don't match the majority of everybody else in the club, we just say, "Is this really for you?" because maybe it's not, and there's nothing wrong with that. When you join the club, you join because it's the right time for both you and the club to be there. After a certain period of time, it may no longer make sense for you to be a part of the club. It's not anything personal. It's not hard feelings. We know life gets in the way, so we just ask you to make that decision, and sometimes people continue and they really step up. Other times, it's like, "You know, you're right. I'm just going to take my money and go do something else with it," and there are no hard feelings about any of that. It's okay that those kinds of things happen.

The club is a living, breathing entity that will go on with or without those Members. We will always pick up new ones.

Q: Am I going to want to hang out with these people?

CHRIS: Some of them.

JASON: Well, if you follow what we just said about how to pick the Members, I mean, that was one of Jan's criteria: "Will I want to hang out with these people?" But I look at it as this group of people could be only about learning to invest. What they're bringing is their energy. We have the same energy. We want to learn. We have the same strategy in terms of the investment club. And as long as we continue to learn, if you hang out with them once a month, communicate during the month, do what you do, I think that's good. But, obviously, it makes it a lot more fun if you actually like them.

CHRIS: You may not choose to hang out with these people much outside of the club, but the thing about it is you have something in common with them. It's like people at work. When you go out to happy hour with people at work, you do it because you've got something you can talk about. You've got something in common. I think that adds to it, and I think you're more likely to hang out with people once you join a club—any kind of club—if you participate. If you're not an active participant, you're not going to care.

JASON: I agree because, I think, besides Jan, I don't think I knew anybody who started out with the club. I mean, I knew them, but I didn't know that much about them. It seems to have worked out.

JAN: I do hang out with some of these people outside of the club as well, but even if I *only* saw them in an investment club, I would feel just as close to them. I really only socialize with a few of them—like, you know, Robert does my hair and we work out, and I invite some of the people to different parties. There are several people in the club I don't hang out with at all outside of the club, but I like them enough there.

CHRIS: But there are other social situations that come out of our friendship and interaction through the club. I've been to an art opening because of one Member of our club. I've been to a book signing party because of somebody else. I've been to a jewelry show because of somebody else. You know, I think it's just different levels of relationships that you have—like you would any place else.

Q: Is this the only place that club Members invest?

JASON: No.

CHRIS: No.

JAN: It is the only place *some* of our club Members invest. I don't know for sure everybody's investment portfolio and what they do. I know what people talk about, and I assume if you're not talking about investing in some other place, then you aren't investing outside of the club, but I know of at least two of our fifteen club Members who do not invest anywhere else other than this. Outside of investing in the club, I have a **SEP IRA**[10] that I rolled over from a **401k**[11], I have a small **Roth IRA**[12] that I started a few years ago, and I invest in real estate.

---

[10] A Simplified Employee Pension Individual Retirement Arrangement (SEP IRA) is a variation of the Individual Retirement Account.

[11] A 401k is a popular type of employer-sponsored retirement plan that lets employees contribute part of their salaries (generally pre-tax), thus saving and investing for the future. Employers can also contribute to their employee's 401k plans. This type of investment has been around since 1978.

[12] A Roth IRA is an individual retirement account that lets people who earn less than $169,000 (for joint tax filers) and $105,000 (for single filers) set aside after-tax income up to a specified amount each year. All future withdrawals from a Roth IRA are tax-free. Nerdy details: It's named for Senator William Roth, Jr., of Delaware and was created as part of the Taxpayer Relief Act of 1997.

JASON: One of the reasons to start an investment club is to gain knowledge and confidence in investing. So if you don't have any investments now, fantastic! Start a club. Start putting away $50 a month. See it grow. Keep going. But my recommendation to you — even to the two Members of our own club who aren't investing anywhere else — is if you can scrape together another $50 a month, start putting it somewhere else.

JAN: That's right.

JASON: And grow it. Use what you're learning here. We'll talk about investment strategies later. The investment strategy for your club may be different than your personal investment strategy, depending on where you're at in life. It probably *will* be different, but this is where you can learn about things even if they're not stocks. They may not be inside the investment strategy of our club, but you can learn about them there and say, "I'll put my money in some of those because I need a more stable investment than just stocks."

CHRIS: Even if you have a company that has a 401k and you're automatically investing into that, you should still invest in something else outside your club.

Even if you're investing in one of the automated

investment[13] services that puts your money just into an **exchange traded fund** where you don't have to think about it. It's totally mindless. Somebody else is doing it for you. Because you're not confident enough to do that yet, put that money there because, if something did happen to the club and the club didn't make as much money as you wanted it to, you will still have your own investment someplace else that you could deal with as well.

The longer I've been in the club, the more I've started investing on my own outside of the club as well. It gets easier over time. I think absolutely people should, but you're not required to.

Things to Remember
- At the most basic level, every Member of the club puts in the same amount of money each month, and the club Members vote on which stocks to

---

[13] Automated investment services have become all the rage for making life simple for people who do not want to pay attention to what they are doing or need help actually saving money. One of our favorite investment services is Betterment. If you are looking for ways to trick yourself into saving more money, that you can eventually roll over into a more complete investment service, check out Digit or Acorns. Both have helped us squirrel away money without even knowing it.

purchase with the money collected from all Members.
- The right people for your club will be the people who are willing to commit to show up and participate for the long haul. You may not know who these people are until they have actually been in the club for a while, and that's totally ok!
- Everyone will bring a different perspective to the club, so don't spend too much time initially trying to figure out if someone would be interested or if they would have something to offer. You never know until people actually get involved what they will be able to do for your club. If you like them enough to hang out with them once a month, let them in!

Homework
- Take out your list of names you came up with in Chapter 1, and see who else you can add. Seriously, just list everyone and don't censor yourself yet. You can edit this list later. Here are some ideas to help you keep going.
    - Go through your social media accounts.
    - Think about the guests who were at the last party you went to.
    - Scan around your office.

- Who do you want to hang out with?
  - Who has some serious smarts?
  - Who always seems to be lucky?
  - Go wild!
- Start thinking about how much money you can invest every month. We chose $50 because that's what people in our group felt comfortable with. We wanted an amount that would not hurt too much and was also large enough so that people felt compelled to participate every month and watch their money grow. You can decide at your first meeting what amount each person will invest, but it's good to have thought this through for yourself so you have a suggested amount to use as a starting point for this discussion.
- What do you think you would contribute, aside from money, to your club? Are you a good researcher? An educator? Motivated? A leader? Start to come up with what you think you would like to contribute. Identifying what kinds of skills or energy you want to contribute will make you more excited about getting started, and your excitement will help create enthusiasm in the people you eventually invite to join!

Chapter 3: Knowledge and Experience

After reading Chapter 2, you now have an expanded list of possible club Members, an idea of where you might like to start for a monthly investment amount, and an outline of the skills and energy contribution you will personally contribute to have your club be a success. Congratulations! You're well on your way, so let's tackle the thing that stops most people from ever starting a club in the first place: the fear that they don't have enough knowledge or experience to make this work. (Spoiler alert: You can do this!)

Q: Do your Members have a lot of investment experience?

CHRIS: In general, most of our Members did not have a lot of investment experience before they joined our club. We have people who had zero investment experience, and we had a few that had some investment experience, but I don't believe any of them had a lot of investment experience.

JAN: We've said this before, but I think it's important to emphasize that it's okay to not have previous experience. You've got to have your entry point somewhere. That's the whole point of the club—you're going to get more knowledge just by showing up and participating.

But knowledge and experience are different. There are a lot of people who have a lot of knowledge but who don't have direct experience. Maybe they read a lot about it or they subscribed to *Money Magazine* or *Kiplinger's* or *The Wall Street Journal* or whatever, and they *know* a lot, but they're not putting it into *action*, and that's when you say, "Put your money where your mouth is." That's what we're really talking about. Are you willing to put your money in something and then vote and be okay with it if you get outvoted? You might really want something, and the rest of the club doesn't. The experience of that is also very important, and it bumps up against knowledge, and they both feed each other.

Q: Can you do this when you don't know anything? What if I don't know anything?

CHRIS: You know, that's kind of how we started, right? None of us really knew what we were doing.

JAN: Yeah.

CHRIS: Together, we figured it out. With *Rich on Fifty*, this book that you've just bought (and for that, we thank you!), you've got all the tools that you need to get it started. So even if you know absolutely nothing, by the time that you're done with this book and the homework that we're assigning you throughout the book, you'll have it made.

JAN: It's also important to push back on what people *say* they know. Sometimes, a Member of our club will make a statement about something they "know", and I'll say, "How do you *know* that?" And they will say, "Well, that's just my gut feeling." "Okay, that's fine, but what are you giving us to back that up? What have you read about that? What do the numbers say?" We encourage you to question your own assumptions and your own knowledge.

I thought I knew a little bit about stocks. Well, I

didn't know anything about P/E ratio or what earnings per share means. All the nitty-gritty stuff, I didn't know. I could have told you a fifth-grader's level of information, maybe but getting deeper? No. My knowledge has definitely deepened since we started the club, and that's as it should be.

It doesn't matter how much you know or how little you know when you start. If you're willing to learn from other people and be open-minded and push back and ask questions and look stupid, then you will learn what you need to learn. We have no trouble asking dumb questions or what other people would think are dumb questions because we want to learn, and that's what we're here for.

JASON: Our investment club started out with a bunch of people who didn't know very much but had an interest in learning, and your investment club may start the same way, or you may have a mix. You may have people who know a lot, who have an interest in sharing as well as learning a few other things and who want to add to their knowledge.

It's not really all that hard. You put some money together, you open a trading account, you buy a stock, you see what happens.

JAN: Right.

CHRIS: It's not that we don't pay attention to gut feelings. It's that, when you're trying to make a decision, you may make a different decision if you know what somebody is telling you is something they *know* versus something they *feel*. We, as human beings, confuse those two things a lot. I have no problem with you telling me, "My gut feeling is that this stock is going to go crashing down in the next two months," but as long as you tell me that's your gut feeling, I'm okay with that, and we may sell it or we may not buy it because of your gut feeling. You just have to be honest and clear with your communications when you're giving information out.

JAN: I think the great equalizer here is everybody puts in the same amount of money and everybody has one vote. It doesn't matter if I have more experience than you; my vote counts the same as yours. It doesn't matter that you "only have $50." That's all I'm putting in, too, in this pot. So your $50 is equal to my $50, and we're putting in the same amount of money. It's not the golden rule. It's not, "I'm putting in more money, therefore, I get to decide what happens in the club." Everybody has an equal vote.

We also, by the way, have Members who are married couples or partners who just put in $50 as a couple, but they still only get one vote.

They both might show up at the meeting and both might do research, but it's still only one vote.

JASON: You made me think of another benefit of joining an investment club, especially for the knowledgeable people, because you've now got ten or fifteen other people that you need to convince as to why the club should buy a particular stock. Maybe you don't do that very well. Maybe you don't communicate very well with people. Maybe you just think, "This is the best stock." You might not know that Tesla (TSLA) is going to be an awesome stock, but if you think it is, you can train yourself in communicating and selling your ideas and your enthusiasm inside of the investment club.

JAN: That's true because, sometimes, people present a stock that looks really good on paper but nobody's excited about it. Well, if you're not excited about it and you presented it, I'm not going to buy it. So you could hone your skills.

Q: Prior to joining the club, what other investment experiences have you had?

CHRIS: I had a 401k and a 403b with previous employers, and I really didn't know what I was doing with it. I just set it to auto-balance, and it picked everything for me, so I didn't really have to work with it at all. But also, I thought investing was something that I should be doing, so I opened up my own trading account, and I started trying to buy my own stocks, and I made some really horrendous decisions because I had nobody to talk to about it to figure it out.

I would do the same things that we've warned about here. I'd go online and read a research study—like, "Oh, this IPO is coming out," and I'd buy whatever I could afford in it, and three months later, it'd tank, and I didn't understand what happened. So, I really had some pretty bad stock trading experiences, and that, again, is one of the reasons I joined the club. I wanted somebody else to talk me off the ledge.

To the people who are reading this book, you've never gone shopping with me, but I am the worst person to go shopping with because I can't make up my mind when I'm trying to buy things. I can talk myself into or out of anything. So, I like to get the advice of other people who can help me. I mean, when it comes down to it, I will pick something, and I will buy it, but I like to have those other voices to help me make sure that my logic is sound and just.

JAN: Well, the beauty, too, of picking stocks—which we're going to talk about in Chapter 9:

Stock Picking—is if the club doesn't vote for the thing you want, you can still invest in it on your own. You can put your $50 or $100 or whatever a month aside until you've got enough money to buy some shares of that, and you can still do it. The club didn't buy it, but you can still buy it.

JASON: In terms of experience, like Chris, I have a 401k through work. And every time I'd get to a new job and sign up for a 401k, they would ask, "Okay, which fund do you want?" I'm like, "Which one is the riskiest? I'll take that one." Because I'm still young. I want some gains at the end. You know, I'm not thinking about retiring any time soon, so I can take a risk. I'd just pick it out. I had no clue what any of the other things meant. I sure couldn't look at all that stuff and really evaluate those funds. Today, I could evaluate all my 401ks' offerings much better than I could have done then. But that was the only investing experience that I had before joining the club.

JAN: My grandmother managed the money in her household, and she invested in some CDs and mutual funds. She didn't buy stock outright, but I remember sitting down with her when I was probably 10 or 11 and asking her to tell me about her investments and to show me about it a little bit—just a very little bit. It was enough for me to be interested, but I didn't really do a whole lot with what she taught me.

And then, when I went into teaching, I had Texas Teacher Retirement (TRS), and you can't direct that at all. It's kind of like social security: you just put the money in, and you hope it comes back to you in the end. But when I left teaching, I was able to take that money out and roll it over into an investment that I could control. It really made me sad that it was only making about 5% a year before that. That is terrible. If I could have directed it like you can direct a 401k, that would have been much more exciting.

I've done stupid things with investments, too. I've taken out money from my Texas Teacher Retirement to pay off some debt. I mean, that's not necessarily stupid, but how much money would I have if it had still been invested? Who knows?

I also had an individual retirement account—an IRA—and I did have a money manager for a little while. I'd go maybe every six months or once a year, and he would say, "I recommend this and this and this." I'd just be like, "Okay, whatever, you're the money guy. You must know what you're doing," and I still felt like he must know a lot and I didn't know anything, so I didn't put any time into really figuring things out. I was just kind of bumbling along.

And then we started this investment club at the end of 2008/beginning of 2009. In 2012, I took a job where I had a 401k for the first time in my life, and I knew enough by then to sock as much money away as I could. I didn't quite do the max but I almost did — it was a big, big chunk of money for two years because I thought, "Well, I've never had this job before, and I've never had this salary before, so I'm not going to miss this money." I was able to put $40,000 aside in two years, including the company match, and the money that it made, so when I left that job and went back to being only self-employed, I took my 401k and I rolled it over into a SEP IRA — a simplified employee pension individual retirement account.

I opened the SEP IRA with E*TRADE because I now have experience buying and selling our club's stocks through that platform. Now I can direct my money based on what I've learned from the investment club, and I can add to it as I wish directly from my business. But it wasn't until I got in the investment club that I had the confidence to really take on my money and my retirement savings and own it like I knew what I was doing.

I've since taken a lot of the money from my SEP

IRA and used it to open a **Solo 401k**[14]. And a few months ago, I took a loan from that account and bought myself a piece of rental property that I'm now Airbnb-ing the hell out of. You never know where your knowledge will take you!

CHRIS: It's important to say, too, that "your mileage may vary". But I guarantee you, if you do the things that we're suggesting that you do in this book, you will look back after 5, 7, 10, or even 20 years, and you will have had a good time and you will have learned something from it.

JASON: Yes.

CHRIS: You may not get the returns that other clubs are getting, but you will come up with something else — that knowledge.

JAN: But if you do get amazing returns, we're going to take credit for that, ha ha!

JASON: Absolutely.

---

[14] A Solo 401(k), (also known as a Self Employed 401(k) or Individual 401(k)), is a 401(k) qualified retirement plan that was designed specifically for employers with no full-time employees other than the business owner(s) and their spouse(s).

Q: How would you rate your investment knowledge now that you've been in the club for several years?

JASON: A nine!

JAN: Out of?

JASON: I don't know.

JAN: Twenty-seven or ten?

JASON: None of us is going to say we know everything. We still purchase stocks that don't make money, and we purchase stocks that make a lot of money. I think the real benefit is that this knowledge has come with experience. We've been able to put those together and, really, the sky's the limit. There are other people in our club who don't know as much as I do because they haven't put the effort into learning that I did or they don't learn like I do. You know, they see a presentation and they don't catch it.

I would say, definitely, my investment knowledge is three or four times what it was before I joined the club.

JAN: Yeah, I would say that, too.

JASON: And, with the information we're giving you here, it could be five or six times.

JAN: Quickly.

CHRIS: Yeah.

I don't know how to answer this other than saying my **net worth**[15] now is more than it was when I joined the club, and that is principally because of the investments I've made since joining the club. It's been more than eight years. Yes, I've had a few raises. Yes, I've changed jobs a few times. That's all true. But the majority of my net worth change is actually because of my investments, not because I changed careers or did something else. I changed what I did with the money that I had by just doing the research. And it's not always just the research for the club and buying stocks. It's while I was on the road to researching a stock, I read somebody's advice on something you should be doing with your money, and I started applying that. There's just a whole lot of other stuff that's all involved.

I would say that, if anybody tells you that they are an expert investor and you should listen to

---

[15] Simply put, your net worth is how much you *own* minus how much you *owe*, which could be a negative or a positive number. Websites such as Mint offer tools that will connect to your bank accounts and creditors, track your assets and liabilities, and calculate this number for you.

their advice—unless that person's name is Warren Buffett—they're lying to you. There's just too much to think about, too much to decide. It's too much for anybody to say that they're an expert in this. But I know that I've got the confidence I'm going to use to continue to increase my net worth. I'm going to continue increasing my investments, and every year that I participate in this club, my knowledge gets stronger.

JAN: Plus, there is the advent—every month practically—of new apps or tools or websites or technology to help you do this. Like Mint and Betterment and…

CHRIS: Acorns.

JAN: Yeah, Acorns. Rich on Fifty.

CHRIS: Digit.

JAN: Exactly. I mean, the fact that these things are available and you have your own investment club, now you're more open to taking advantage of them and using your knowledge to leverage the little bit of knowledge you had before. It's just like investing. You're investing in yourself but with the knowledge and the time that you're putting into the club. You're going to see that "diagonal up" line in your investment knowledge.

CHRIS: Up and to the right.

JAN: Up and to the right!

JASON: All of us in the club are about the same age, and we're eventually going to retire. I don't know when we're going to retire, but I've always thought that social security may not be there when I retire. It may be there; it may not be. Honestly, if you don't take control of your money now, then when you're 60, 70, or 80, you may not have any. You may be working at Walmart as a greeter, not because you want to get out and be sociable—though I'm sure a lot of people do it that way—but because you need to buy food and put it on the table. This goes back to the why of being in an investment club: learning the knowledge and taking control of your financial future is a very important step for you to take.

Things to Remember
- In order to start an investment club, you do not need to have any prior knowledge! The most important thing you bring to the table is enthusiasm and the desire to learn.
- It is ok if each Member of your club comes with different levels of experience.

Each Member will bring their own experiences to the club, which will ultimately help it grow.

Homework

- It's time to take stock (ha!) of your investment knowledge! Go ahead and rate yourself right now. When it comes to stocks, is your knowledge level:
    - **Novice:** You know how to spell the word "stock" and that's about it;
    - **Intermediate:** You know where to look them up and you can throw around some basic financial terms;
    - **Advanced:** You toss around those financial terms like a boss and know not only where to look a stock up but also how to read what is listed for each stock; or
    - **Expert:** You are like the **Oracle of Omaha**[16] and can divine the trends of a stock by licking your finger and sticking it in the air. (Though that's *not* how the Oracle does it!)
- What is your past experience with investing? Jot down a couple paragraphs detailing whatever kind of investment experience you have. Make sure to list

---

[16] https://en.wikipedia.org/wiki/Warren_Buffett

some of the greatest things you have done and some of your biggest mistakes.
- It is also very helpful to write about your family's experience with money and investing. Looking at where you come from and the stories you have brought with you about what it means to be rich or poor, to have money or not have it, will make a difference in your confidence and your success with money now and in the future. Do you have a "never enough" story about money? Where did that come from? What happened in your life or your family to put that story there?
- List out all of the financial accounts you have, if you have any, and what kind they are. (For example, checking account, savings account, 401k, 403b, IRA, Roth IRA, SEP IRA, etc.)
- **BONUS POINTS:** Calculate your net worth.
- **SUPER BONUS POINTS:** Input all of your assets and liabilities into the tools on Mint[17] and really get clear about your financial picture. And don't stress! You can't improve your position until you know where you're starting from.

---

[17] https://www.mint.com/

Chapter 4: Operations

By now, you've had some time to think about your skill level, consider investing outside your club (or maybe you already do), and stepping up your investing game. Kudos to you if you took on the "above and beyond" assignment of putting your accounts into Mint.com to calculate and track your net worth. Don't have a net worth yet? Don't worry! This is why you're here.

Let's turn our attention now to the successful operation of your club, which is the next step in getting educated about stock investing. Who knows where you'll go from here?

JAN: So, let's talk about the boring stuff first.

Q: What are the legal things that we have to do to start an investment club?

CHRIS: The biggest hurdle that you're going to have to overcome is creating bylaws for your club because you're going to need those in order to open up your investment club brokerage account.

We're going to walk you through exactly how to create those bylaws because it took us months to come up with them, and we really didn't understand what we were saying, but we finally came up with a set of bylaws that are pretty comprehensive. They're easy to read, they're easy to understand, and they will cover you. That is going to knock off a lot of time for getting your club up and running. I can't stress enough how important it is for you to have these bylaws written because it explains how your club operates regarding the things that you don't want to talk about all day—like, how many club Members can we add? How much money do they have to put in? When does the money have to be there? What do we do if somebody leaves? What do we do if somebody dies? All that stuff is taken care of once, and you're good for the rest of the time.

JAN: As part of our Rich on Fifty courses, we are creating templates for you to do all that.

Q: What else do we have to do, legally?

JASON: Well, you must legally form a partnership with the state. And, legally, we did have to get a tax ID number[18].

JAN: We did.

JASON: I don't believe there was anything "legal" other than getting that tax ID number and signing a general partnership agreement, but you can actually legally file papers with your state, with the government, saying, "This is our partnership."

But if you ever think you want to start being Warren Buffett and having people give you money so your investment club can invest that money, then you'll need to be doing something like that.

CHRIS: There are advantages and disadvantages to forming a company or a corporation or an LLC or an LLP or whatever else you want to do. We're not going to go through that because if you want to go to those lengths to protect yourself—and maybe you should, especially if you're putting in a lot of money, you've got a lot of assets, and you may want more protection than what we're going to teach you how to do—then you should go to a professional and get that done. For the best advice for where you live, contact the local office

---

[18] An EIN, or Employer Identification Number.
https://www.irs.gov/businesses/small-businesses-self-employed/employer-id-numbers-eins

of a brokerage, who may even have the paperwork for you, or an attorney.

JAN: Disclaimer: We are not attorneys!

JASON: Yet.

Q: What kinds of records should our club be keeping?

CHRIS: You definitely need to have agendas and meeting minutes for your club because there have been a lot of times when we've ended up researching the same stock multiple times because nobody could remember what we researched in previous meetings, or there were no minutes available for somebody to go back and look at when they were doing their research.

JAN: Or people were absent when a stock was presented and didn't know it had been, so they repeated the research that had already been done a few months before.

JASON: And obviously, you need to keep track of how much money people send to the club, when they send it in, and what stocks you're buying and when you buy them. And you should be keeping financial records because if you don't know how well you're doing or how well your stock picks are doing, you can't progress and grow and get better at this.

JAN: You also want to keep attendance records. That seems really basic, but our club has a statement in our bylaws about this because we don't want people to miss more than four meetings in a year. We meet monthly, and if people come to at least eight meetings, we assume that they are still participating and still involved.

We realize some people have to travel a lot for work. One of our club Members is in the military reserves, so sometimes he is gone unexpectedly when we have club meetings. Paying attention to who's coming to each meeting will help you when it's time to possibly deselect a Member from your club or at least talk to people to ascertain their level of continued interest and participation. You could say, "You know, I've noticed you haven't been here the last three meetings. Are you still interested in being an active Member?"

Another problem that we had early on was people giving notice at the last minute — "Oh, by the way, I'm not coming today" — for a meeting that starts in an hour. That's totally uncool because you need a quorum to make a decision, and if you don't have a majority of your people there — according to whatever your bylaws say your quorum requirements are — you can't make an official decision to trade, and on a Membership of 15 people, for example, you've wasted the time of six people when nine people didn't show up.

CHRIS: You should also keep records of the stocks that you've researched and keep copies of all that research in case you want to go back and look at it again.

JAN: Yes, we file away all of our information in two different ways. We started out creating individual stock folders in Yahoo, and now we have a club Dropbox[19] folder. Your club will need to decide what works best for you, but if it is cloud-based, everyone can add to it and access it, even if one person is ultimately responsible for maintaining it. In our club, it's the Vice President, which (at the time of this writing) is me. You might have a different platform where you want to keep that information.

Q: Who's in charge and how did you decide that?

JASON: Jan's in charge because that's just how she rolls!

---

[19] This is a link to the Dropbox website, NOT our club's Dropbox folder! https://www.dropbox.com/

JAN: It's "my" club. Okay, not really—I just started it. But I *do* really feel ownership—in a good way!

Actually, we have officers. Your club will need to determine the appropriate activities for each of your officers and codify their role description and their term in your bylaws so you have that to refer to. We have a President, a Vice President, a Secretary, and a Treasurer, and their roles are as follows:

1. **President:**
   - Presides at all club meetings;
   - Appoints Members to the Audit Committee (and usually serves on it him/herself);
   - Works with the Secretary to prepare the meeting agendas;
   - Is authorized to handle financial transactions and make trades in the club's online brokerage account;
   - Comes up with brilliant ideas for how the club can function more efficiently or get back on track;
   - Breathes new life into club operations on a regular basis.

2. **Vice President:**
   - Takes the place of the President when he is absent, which is rarely;
   - Organizes the annual scheduling of research for the club and communicates it to the Secretary (each club Member is required to research and present at least one stock twice annually, so SOMEBODY'S gotta enforce this!);
   - Makes sure the Treasurer has executed the trades (buy or sell) that we agreed to in the club meetings (and makes them herself if the Treasurer forgets or is absent from the meeting);
   - Organizes the Dropbox folder that holds all club research and grants new Members access to the folder;
   - Coordinates the club's education program (and delivers most of the program herself or delegates it to other officers); and
   - Is authorized to handle financial transactions and make trades in the club's online brokerage account.

3. **Secretary:**
   - Notifies Members of regular meetings;
   - Reminds Members who is researching what and when;
   - Keeps minutes of all club meetings (which mostly consists of attendance and stocks purchased); and

- Works with the President to prepare and send out the meeting agenda.

4. **Treasurer:**
   - Keeps the club's books, which includes reconciling club Members' deposits between the brokerage account and the club's accounting software and noting which deposit is attributable to which Member;
   - Sends out a report (typically screenshots) of the portfolio's value via email a few days before each meeting;
   - Ensures the club's accounting software has completed individual and club tax reports (K1s[20]) and distributes these to each Member to file with their personal taxes (typically late February);
   - Helps new Members get set up for monthly deposits to the club's online brokerage account; and
   - Is authorized to handle financial transactions and make trades in the club's online brokerage account.

We started out just by asking who wanted to

---

[20] Schedule K-1 is a tax document used to report the incomes, losses, and dividends of a partnership. The K-1 document is prepared for each individual partner and is included with the partner's personal tax return.

have an officer role. The roles have changed a little bit over time. I was Treasurer at the very beginning just because it was my idea to start the club, and I was willing to go to the E*TRADE office and keep track of all of that. It's important to note that I was not a stellar Treasurer, but I was interested enough in it to volunteer, and then I served a small stint as Secretary, which I thought I would have been good at, but really, I was kind of lousy. Now, I'm very excited to be the Vice President because I like that role a lot more than the other roles. We do have four officers, and we vote each January on the new club officers, and those people serve one-year terms.

Now, in our ninth year of being a club, we have had several people who have been officers for most of those years — if not all of them — and we, as a club, definitely want to actively cultivate people to take over those roles in the coming year because I don't need to serve an officer term every year. I don't mind doing it, but I also want to give other people the opportunity to grow and develop themselves in the club and to get the confidence that you get from exercising that responsibility. Admittedly, some people don't want that or they don't have time for it, and that's fine, but I don't want to just hog up all the roles all the time.

CHRIS: It really depends on the club that you're

joining or starting because I've been in clubs before where, like ours, there aren't a lot of people who are stepping up and wanting to take on the responsibility or the time commitment to be an officer in the club. We are trying to make this a very dedicated club that's extremely active, and that takes a little bit more time to do. The fact is, there are only a few people who are really interested in serving in officer roles, but it's not a big deal.

There are other clubs that I've been in where it's two men enter, one man leaves. I mean, it's a fight to the death to see who gets to be which officer, and people really duke it out, but I think it really just depends on the club and the group of people that you've brought on board.

JAN: So far, people have been very amenable to, "Oh, you want to do that? Okay, great, we'll vote for you to do that." We haven't had any internal dissention about that, but I do want to encourage other Members to step up even when it's uncomfortable for them to do so because I think that that would be good for them, but they do get to choose.

JASON: We've talked about this a little bit in our officer group this year, and I'm actually really excited because it could look like next year I'm not an officer.

JAN: You should be grooming somebody to take your position.

JASON: Yes, someone else could be doing this, and while I enjoy being an officer, it does take some time and effort, and you have to grow that club leadership because, as an officer, let me tell you, you're going to learn more. You're going to know more. You're going to be the ones who, when you say, "Hey, we should buy this stock," people are going to listen to you more. If you grow that knowledge throughout the whole club, your club just gets better.

Q: What are the biggest challenges the club faces when putting together an agenda?

JASON: Following it.

JAN: Agenda? We didn't even *have* an agenda for a little while. Our agenda has morphed over time.

CHRIS: Yeah, we've matured as a club. But now we have a pretty standard agenda that we try to follow, and even if you have one, you won't always follow it. That's okay. But we're really trying to stick to it because we think that it covers the stuff that we do—the things we think are important to touch on month after month.

But there are two challenges to putting them together.

One is making sure that the educational topic you've picked to cover that month is a topic that is interesting and relevant and that people are going to learn from — and that you assign that topic to somebody who can thoroughly research it and is prepared to explain it, and that can be one person or it could be several people. If you want to do that in pairs, that's great, too. There are lots of different ways you can do that, but deciding on the educational topic is a big one.

The other challenge is that there is always a little dissention when you're trying to figure out what other things to cover because — especially when you talk about people's money — there's always a little pet thing that somebody wants to get in. Like, for years, we've had somebody every month say, "I want to cover how we're going to sell stocks and when we should do that." And so, it ends up on the agenda over and over again, but for a long time, no one was really willing to actually take it on and cover it.

JASON: I think that the person who brings it up should cover it.

CHRIS: Yet we never actually covered it for all

that time[21], so should we have put it on the agenda if we didn't really have anybody who was willing to take it on? The answer, I think, is yes, but we needed more commitment from Members to take on responsibility for education and coming up with new ideas.

JAN: At our website, richonfifty.com, you can access a downloadable document with an outline for your club's first year (it's also in the book appendix), complete with suggestions for educational pieces. We walk you through the whole process of getting started, getting set up, getting your documents together, and yes, it will take you a couple of months before you're ready to buy a stock as a club, but we walk you through all of that, too, so that you don't have to

---

[21] We've covered it now! This became an increasingly bigger topic as the years went on at Stocks and Bondage; we originally had in our manifesto that we would be getting rich slowly, so we hesitated to sell anything and opted to hold things for the long term. Like most human beings, we had a few moments of panic where we sold some stocks that, in hindsight, we probably should not have sold. We also did not sell some stocks we probably should have.

You can read more about our process in Chapter 9.

This is not something you probably want to do until you have a few years under your belt, but getting started with the process of reviewing the poor performers is good to take on from the beginning. We also stopped selling our bottom performers when we felt, as a group, that our portfolio was manageable.

wonder, "Are we ready? Do we know enough? We don't know enough! We can't buy anything!" No, just follow our menu for twelve months, and you'll have a successful first year.

JASON: We've had many meetings over our eight-plus years where we didn't have a formal agenda at all. We just walked in and winged it. I'm going to tell you, during those years, the club wasn't as fun, and we did not make as good returns. We bought stocks that we shouldn't have bought—more so in those years than in years where we've been focused on exactly what we were going to do and what we were going to learn—and that really requires a club leader to step up and say, "Here is the agenda." If you're worried about bossing people around, don't be. That's what everyone is there for. They're there to learn. They're there to see these things grow, and it helps to have a road map to follow.

Q: So, what about the tax implications of this? Are there any?

JASON: Yes, there are. Every time you sell a stock, you earn money or you lose money, and there are two different types of tax implications. One is a short-term capital gain, and the other one is a long-term capital gain. Basically, the difference is the length of time (one year). If you own it for less than a year, it's short-term. Long-term is if you own it for more than a year.

If you're going to follow our philosophy which is "buy and hold" — you buy good companies so that, even if the stock goes down, you know it has performed well in the past well, and you feel confident that it is eventually going to go back up — you're not going to do a lot of selling. So the tax implications for a $50-a-month investment club work out to, over the years, I think it's affected my taxes, at the most, two or three dollars.

The numbers on this graph are based on actual capital gains realized by one Member of our investment club. Remember, you only realize gains when you sell stock, so our portfolio was increasing in value, while our gains appear low.

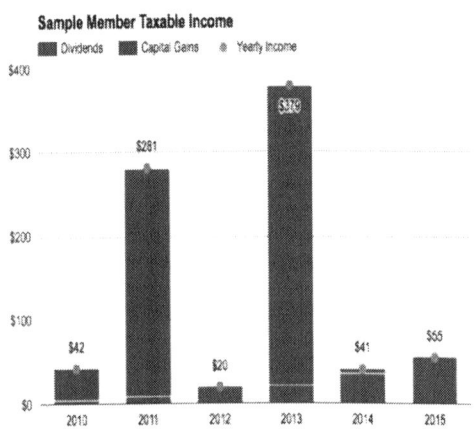

Max yearly income: $379. Minimum yearly income: $20. Average yearly income: $136.

CHRIS: A good thing to remember here is that, just as you put in money every month and you get a share of the assets of the company, when the company sells stocks, you only take a share of the losses and the profits, which in general are very small (and the share of them is even smaller).

For example, if there are ten people in your club and your club sold stocks that made a profit of $100 over the course of the year, your tax implication is that it only raised your income by $10 ($100 divided by 10 Members).

JAN: It's not going to push you into the next tax bracket—or down.

CHRIS: Exactly.

JASON: If it does, find another deduction—quick!

CHRIS: At the rate we're telling you to invest, $50 a month, the tax implications are going to be very low—very, very low. The exception, of course, is when you take all of your money out of the club. Then you may be hit with a heavier than normal tax situation.

JAN: But it is important to point out there is a tax responsibility. The club accounting software does produce what's called a K1, which shows each individual Member and the amount of money attributed to their performance relative to the shares that they own of the overall club. You do have to file your Schedule K1 with your personal income tax. That is your tax responsibility. But the tax implications are very minimal, if anything at all. There's no big swing in your income or gain or loss based on what you're doing in the club. We're not day-trading.

CHRIS: And remember, this isn't Rich on Fifty Thousand. It's Rich on Fifty.

JAN: Dollars!

CHRIS: The club does have to file a tax return every year. It's not just the K1. You have to file the tax return, and each individual Member gets a K1. If this is all confusing for you, that's fine. There are many resources available around the web, or you can contact any tax preparer for advice.

JASON: Disclaimer: we're not tax professionals!

JAN: Yet...

Things to Remember

- To run a legal club, you need to make sure you form an actual investment club. In many states, this can be a basic partnership agreement that is handed over to the brokerage of your choice when you are opening up your account.
- Be sure to keep accurate records of your income and expenses, including:
    - What stocks you purchased, when you purchased them, and how much you spent;
    - What other services you subscribed to; and
    - How much money each person contributed.
- You will have to file a tax return for your club. Fortunately, there are many options for taking care of club accounting that can walk you through filing the correct paperwork.
- It is a good idea to have a defined agenda for each of your meetings to keep the club moving forward.
- Having officers ensures that there are people in place who are responsible for organizing the club and making sure any legal and financial deadlines are met.

Homework

- Find a copy of a simple partnership agreement that you can modify and use for your investment club.
- Create a list of the officers you think you might need, and what duties those officers may need to perform every month.
- Brainstorm a list of stock related terms that you are unfamiliar with and assign them to potential months of the year. This is to get you to start thinking about topics for your meetings.

Chapter 5: Running a Meeting

Now that you know the basics for getting up and running, it is time to look at what it takes to run an actual meeting. Consider this outline a good starting point for your club's structures and modify according to your needs.

The format of this chapter is different from the rest of the book and should be used as a handy reference tool going forward. See also Your Club's First Year for 12-month outline of Club Business, Education Topics, and Homework.

Preparation

Before each meeting, the Officers should prepare as follows:

- **President:** Set agenda and send to Secretary
- **Vice President:** Ensure the education topic is ready to present
- **Secretary:** Distribute minutes from last meeting; send out agenda for upcoming meeting

- **Treasurer:** Reconcile transactions between the club accounting software and online brokerage account; prepare and distribute the portfolio summary document (we email screenshots to all Members)

Suggested Agenda Format

Go to **www.richonfifty.com/resources/** to download this table as a PDF.

TOPIC	WHO?	DETAILS
Attendance	Secretary	Ensure quorum in accordance with your bylaws. For example, in our club, we must have two-thirds of the Members present in order to conduct business.
Approve Minutes	Secretary	For us, this means a quick vote of approval to make sure we recorded last month's business correctly regarding attendance and other issues and which stocks we bought and sold.
Review Portfolio	Treasurer	In our meetings, we use Chromecast or Apple TV to project research, web pages, and other presentations from a Member's iPad to the meeting location's television screen, but

TOPIC	WHO?	DETAILS
		you could rely on laptops, projectors, or even paper copies. Whatever works for you.
Stock Updates	Members	In our club, each stock we purchase is assigned to a Member to "own". In subsequent meetings, Members give updates on "their" stocks every quarter. Some things we usually cover are news about the company, stock trends, or any other interesting pieces of information, positive or negative, that the Member has researched. Setting up a Google Alert on "your" stocks will keep you up to date and in the know when it's your turn to talk about the stock assigned to you.
Education	Vice President	While the Vice President is responsible for club education, any Member may deliver the training content. To share the workload and improve the education process for all Members, try having the club as a whole decide on a topic and determine who will take on presenting it.

TOPIC	WHO?	DETAILS
		Use Dropbox, Google Docs, or another platform of your choice to keep track of all of the topics that have been covered each month. Refer new Members to this resource, and review them as needed as a club.
Present Research	Members	Researching stocks is how everyone learns and gains confidence. Each January, our Secretary manages the process by which Members choose 2-3 months when they will research and present stocks to the club. We aim to have at least 2 Members presenting stocks each month so we have several to choose from. When presenting stocks to the club, we ask that each presenting Member have at least one stock to present that they would personally recommend the club buy. (It's not enough to show up and say, "I researched four stocks and didn't like any of them." The goal of the club is to BUY STOCKS.)
Voting	President	We (almost) follow Robert's

TOPIC	WHO?	DETAILS
	(Presents) Secretary (Records) Treasurer (Buys/ Sells)	Rules of Order in nominating stocks to be purchased from among those presented that month. Once a stock has been nominated, if another Member seconds, the President calls for a vote. Our club bylaws state that "majority rules", so if at least 50% of the club votes to buy the stock, the Secretary records that the stock was approved for purchase, and the Treasurer places the buy order immediately after. (Our club meets on Sunday, so the trade does not take place until the market opens the following day.)
Any Other Business	President	If there are any other club topics that need to be discussed, the President will open up the discussion.
Complete the Meeting	President	Announce the date, time, and location of the next meeting. Confirm and record any known absences in advance. Remind everyone who is

TOPIC	WHO?	DETAILS
		doing research at the next meeting. Reconfirm the next education topic and which Member will be presenting it.

Things to Remember

- Although these are your friends and acquaintances and this *is* a "club", it's important to remember that you are conducting actual business with monetary implications. You need structures, and an agenda provides that structure. So do officer roles.
- If you've never heard of Roberts Rules of Order (or any sort of parliamentary procedure), take some time to get familiar. You don't have to follow someone else's rules exactly—there's no Rich on Fifty investment club police or anything—but it *is* very important to work out a system of discussing one thing at a time, voting on that one thing, and then moving on to the next item without mixing up the discussion with the vote. That will only lead to confusion, and your Members won't take the votes seriously if there is confusion. You need a procedure

that you follow every single time there is a meeting, a discussion, and a vote. ("Is there any discussion on this item before we vote?" "I move that we…" "I second that motion." "Who is in favor?" "Who is against?" "Who is abstaining?" and so forth.)
- Be sure you are recording votes, purchases, and other decisions so you have a record of what happened when and who was present/absent, etc.

Homework

- Decide on the first format for your club's agenda and the method you will use to keep records (paper, electronic, Google Doc, a document in Dropbox, or some cool app we don't even know about).
- Try out your draft agenda at the next meeting, then debrief what worked, what didn't work, and how you should tweak it for the next meeting. It will probably take you 2-3 meetings to get a system you like and that works well.

Chapter 6: Money and Cost

WOW! You're moving right along! Now you've formed a partnership, registered your club, gotten an EIN, and started keeping records. You've also elected officers and started drafting a club agenda to keep your group on track. LOOK AT YOU! You're doing GREAT, so let's keep it going. This chapter will address your club's expenses.

Q: What are the typical club expenses that you could expect?

CHRIS: There's really not that much. You've got the expense of whatever you're using to keep track of the accounting, and that can be as easy as using Excel or even pen and paper. There's no real need to have any kind of expense for that, but you can and that can range anywhere from free to $279[22].

---

[22] bivio, for example, has three levels of subscription services. At the time of publication, they were $149, $179, and $279. Unless you're in a state with a personal income tax, you'll likely only need the first level of services. For more information, https://www.bivio.com/site/bp/Services.

If you choose to have an accountant do your taxes at the end of the year, that might cost you another $250 or so, but again, you could use some accounting packages for club accounting that do that for you as part of the annual fee.

Q: How do you decide to pay those expenses? Who pays them?

CHRIS: We pay them out of the club budget. Everybody's $50 a month goes into the club's brokerage account, and we know that at least once a year we're going to pay some kind of accounting service for that cost.

JASON: When we started out, we upped our January payment by $25 to cover this cost, so everyone paid $75 that month.

CHRIS: Yes, that's right.

JASON: It was to cover the accounting cost for the year. Now we are in our ninth year, and we don't do that anymore because it was kind of a hassle to make sure people got that extra money in the account. Once you put your $50 on auto-pay, it's just automatic and you don't have to go in and jack with it. Making sure that eight or ten or fifteen people get their extra $25 in wasn't worth the hassle. It's just easier to take it out of the money that we would buy a stock with, and we just do it once a year.

Our E*TRADE account has a debit card associated with it, so we just use that, and the money comes out of our club funds.

Q: Can I afford this?

CHRIS: I don't know if you can or not. I don't know what your monthly budget is, but for us, it really is only $50. We say "Rich on Fifty," but it doesn't have to be $50. If your club is full of people who can't afford $50 a month and you need to start smaller, you could do $10 a month. If you want to do $150 a month, you could do that.

When we were discussing the club, we proposed a lot of different options, and we came to a price that most people in the club thought that they could do.

JAN: I think $50 is important as opposed to $10 — for me, anyway — because, at $50 a month, it's not an amount I'm really going to miss, but it's enough money that it makes me interested and want to go to the meetings because I know we're going to be able to spend $500 at a time on stocks and so I'm a little more invested in it — pardon the pun — than I would be at $10 a month. But, you're right, anybody could start at any point and then move up. I think the main thing is $50 is not something most people are really going to miss in a month. In any 30-day period, you probably spend that much on Starbucks or on going out to dinner just once, so it's really not that much money.

JASON: You need to get with your club and decide what that range is. For some people, that much money might be $20. For some people, $50 might be what they tip the valet driver every night. So, you want it be enough that it gets your attention—so it at least has you saying, "Okay, if I lose every penny of this, I'm not going to like it, but I'm not going to be destitute and on the street, but it is enough to make me pay attention, go to the meetings, learn something, and grow it from there."

JAN: The other thing about that is, if $50 is not very much money for you, then great! Go and invest more of your money somewhere else. You don't have to invest everything in the club. The idea is that the $50 is your tuition for learning what you're learning with the club, so it's worth it to me to pay $50 a month just to get the knowledge that I'm getting. The bonus is that we're also making some money. Invest elsewhere above your $50 club contribution if you can. And even if you have to start small there, that's okay. Just start!

CHRIS: I agree, and Jan's latte example was a really good one, too, because, if you think about the number of lattes it would take you to invest in that club, at the end of the month, you have nothing to show for those lattes. But at the end of ten years of being in an investment club, you sure as hell have a lot to show for what *would* have been those lattes. It's just a different way of thinking about it. Instead of getting an instant gratification, that quick sugar and caffeine high, you're going to have a much bigger return on your investment in the future.

JAN: I can't believe we are already into our ninth year!

CHRIS: I can't either.

JAN: That's fun, how time flies!

Q: Is the money that I put into this club mine? Whose money is this?

JASON: Yes, it's yours.

There are different services out there you can use to track it, but the money you put in is yours. You're buying a portion of the shares that the club buys. If you have ten people in your group and you're each putting in the exactly the same amount of money at the exactly the same time, each of you would own 10% of the shares. If one of you wanted to leave the club and you have a $10,000 portfolio, your portion is $1,000, and the money you put in is yours.

JAN: It's important to note that the software programs that track investments take everything into account. Not to get too hair-splitting here but if I put $50 on the first of the month and Chris puts in $50 on the 15th and Jason puts in $50 on the 30th, technically, it's going to be a little bit different ownership because the stock has gone up or down in the two weeks that's between the two or three purchases.

The reason that we have club accounting software (we use bivio[23]) is so the software can sync with our E*TRADE account and do all of the math on the little nuances of increases and decreases in the club's portfolio value because any and all of those stocks can swing wildly in the space of a day or a week and certainly in a month. It is good to know that the software knows exactly how much money you have put into the account and when it went in relative to the price of the stock and the market activity and

---

[23] https://www.bivio.com/

relative to the club's portfolio total. And if you should need to leave the club, you can take your money out, and everyone has online access so they can know exactly how much their portion is worth. Of course, we would have to sell some things, most likely, to cash you out, especially if you've been here a long time and you've got thousands of dollars in the club account. We might have to sell things as opposed to just reimburse you with cash on hand. But it is important to know that your money is always yours.

Q: So, how rich can I get here?

CHRIS: You can get rich in whatever way you consider "rich" to be. If you consider that being rich in knowledge, you'll be rich in knowledge — incredibly rich — as long as you participate. If you don't put much money in, you won't get financially rich, but it really depends on your goals and what you think is going to happen.

JAN: Oseola McCarty's story is a great — and true — example of this[24]. She was an elderly washerwoman who had worked her whole life taking in laundry and ironing for not much money, just like her mother and grandmother did. But she saved all she could, and at the end

---

[24]http://www.philanthropyroundtable.org/almanac/hall_of_fame/oseola_mccarty

of her life, she had $280,000 in the bank. The woman who had dropped out of school after the sixth grade gave $150,000 of her life savings to the University of Southern Mississippi so complete strangers could get a college education, saying, "I'm giving it away so that the children won't have to work so hard, like I did." This amazing, selfless act inspired others, in turn. More than 600 donors added another $330,000 to her original gift, and Ted Turner, a multibillionaire, was moved to give a billion dollars to charity because of one woman's selfless gift.

And she's not the only unlikely hero or heroine of investing who just kept putting in a little bit at a time and made some smart investments. There are others as well, but the moral of the story here is that a little bit over time adds up to quite a bit of money.

That's the whole point of this Rich on Fifty. If you just drip it in and focus on that and don't panic—just hold on—over time you will certainly be much richer than you would be had you not done anything at all. What you choose to do with those riches is completely up to you.

JASON: The other thing is—let's be honest—at $50, unless you get some really crazy returns and you really hold everything, you're not going to retire on $50 a month unless you're 18 right now.

JAN: That is true.

JASON: All of us here — Chris, Jan, and I — recommend doing additional investing outside of your investment club. Yes, our club portfolio is worth way more than the money we put in it, but even more significant is that we have much more knowledge and experience and confidence in making investment decisions.

CHRIS: That's right. Where we're getting rich is we're taking the knowledge and resources that we've gained through our participation in our investment club and applying that to our own investments outside of the club. That's important to get.

JAN: Yes, and $50 is a great starting point. $50 a month this year, maybe $100 a month next year, maybe $200 after that. Just *start*.

Q: What kind of returns should somebody in an investment club look forward to?

JASON: Our club has continuously outperformed the S&P 500 in the last couple of years — except for the years where we weren't paying a lot of attention. In those years, we pretty much mirrored the S&P.

Here's our club's performance for 2015. We're the green (top) line. The S&P 500 index is the blue (bottom) line. See the chart below, too, for specific gains and losses by months and quarters.

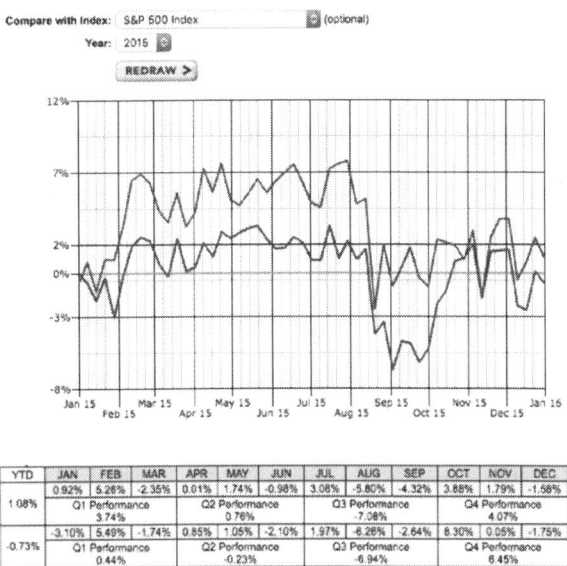

CHRIS: A good way to answer that question is, "It depends." It just depends on how risky your club is willing to be—how willing you are to invest in stable stocks or risky stocks. If we had invested solely in Exxon Mobil (XOM) stocks since our inception and we put $50 per person per month in Exxon Mobil every year, the only real increase we would have had is through our dividends every quarter. But we didn't do that. We took bigger risks. We bought into some new technologies. We invested in some utilities that were kind of cutting-edge and we gained that way.

The returns that you should expect depend on what you want to do (and what you are *actually* doing), and there is an average. Since its inception, the stock market, over time, grows a certain percentage every year[25]. If you're just casually investing, you should expect that level of return. But if you're really active and you're really participating and really studying and learning, then you should be able to beat that average, I think.

Things to Remember
- It is important to keep track of how much money each person pays in every month. This way, you can accurately show how

---

[25] The S&P 500 gauges the performance of the stocks of the 500 largest, most stable companies in the Stock Exchange. It is often considered the most accurate measure of the stock market as a whole. The current average annual return from its inception in 1928 through 2014 is approximately 10%.

much of the club, and your total investments, a club Member owns.
- The amount of money it is possible to make really depends on the club, how well your stocks perform, and how much money you feel comfortable contributing every month.

Homework

- Look at your own spending—no, REALLY look—and see what you could cut out in favor of an additional investment outside your club. Could you start with $25 a month? $50? $250? What could you give up today that would pay off handsomely for you in the future?
- **BONUS POINTS:** Investigate your options for savings and retirement (Traditional IRA? Roth IRA?), and open up your own online brokerage account. Direct a set amount of money there each pay period, and in a few months, when you have the confidence gained from your club's trades and successes, you can start making trades on your own.

Look at you! You're halfway through the book! GOOD JOB!

We assume you like what you're reading so far—at least we hope you do. If that's the case, **please review our book on Amazon** (amazon.com) and let us (and other readers) know what you are learning and what's exciting you. Hey, you might even see your review posted on our web site!

Love Goodreads? We do, too! You can find us on that great site as well. **Leave us some Goodreads love** (goodreads.com) and inform your fellow readers about what they're missing.

We really appreciate your time!

Chapter 7: Risk

Admit it: you're excited now! You're thinking of how you can get rich in knowledge AND in money, and you've even thought about what kind of legacy you could leave for your kids, your spouse or partner, or your community with a steady drip of money invested well over the next ten or twenty years. Best of all, you're committed. You're setting aside the funds, and you're thinking how you can increase that amount to reach your goals. You're looking sexier by the chapter! Now let's talk about how much risk you're willing to take.

Q: How trustworthy are these people in the investment club? Can they or will they steal my money?

JAN: Our club limits the number of people who have direct access to our club's online account. We're happy to show the portfolio to the club at any time or take screenshots of transactions, reports, or charts, but only two or three people have the password to it because, while I trust everybody in the club, there could very well be people who might go in and do something accidentally. You just never know, and it pays to be safe.

Just like you don't want *everybody* to have a key to your house, you don't want *everybody* in the club to have the password to your club's online account. We do change the password to our E*TRADE account every now and then but really, the only people who really care much about it are the officers. Certainly, the Treasurer needs it so he or she can get in make trades or handle whatever else needs to happen. You might want to limit access to just your club's officers or even to just two of them for now. It's always good to have a backup person who knows how to get in and get around.

CHRIS: It's not just that we're happy to provide that information when anybody asks. We're obligated to because it is your right as a Member of the club to see the books at any time—to see the history of purchases, of sales, of current accounting of any of the books at any time that you want to. Maybe you're joining a club or you're creating a club and you only really know one or two of the people well. Although I did not do this, I could have, at every meeting, asked for a copy of the club accounts until I felt comfortable that my money was being managed appropriately.

JAN: We like to give everyone peace of mind by

providing monthly screenshots of our entire portfolio as it appears on E*TRADE, and our Members can also sign in to our online accounting software (which syncs with E*TRADE) with their own password to see how much their portion of the entire portfolio is worth, to see that their deposits have been correctly attributed, and to see what trades have actually been made and when.

Q: How risky is this, really?

JASON: It's the stock market. It's 100% at risk.

JAN: That's right. We have bought stocks that we've lost 100% — literally. I'm thinking of ECOtality. The company went bankrupt, and we now have nothing left from the $500 we invested other than the sad little line on our brokerage statement. On the other end of the spectrum, we have stocks that have increased 100%, 200%, 400%, even 1,000%. No lie! It's a rollercoaster. It's risky. There's nothing guaranteed. Again, you are paying for the knowledge, and your club has to decide how risky you want to be with each individual stock, which then gives you the big picture of risk for your overall portfolio.

CHRIS: If you open a savings account at a bank, there's almost zero risk in doing that, but there's also almost zero reward. I can open a savings account and I can get an interest rate of 0.2% — maybe even 0.02% now, I don't even know. It's so low, it's just not even worth doing. So, yeah, my money might be "safe" because the bank is holding onto it, but I might as well just be putting that under my mattress at that point. There's just not really any upside to it. Shawn Roe has a great graph and explanation of this on his website[26].

We assume you are interested in being in an investment club because you want to make some money with your money. You have to understand that there is some risk involved but there sure is a lot of reward in the long-term. This is not a short game. It's a long game.

JASON: That is one of the things that you will discuss as a club is risk. What is your risk tolerance? As an investor, if you're 22 and you're actually investing to retire, you should have a pretty high-risk tolerance because, if you lose everything, you've still got many more years to go to make it up. If you're 64, you should have a pretty low-risk tolerance because the number of years you have until retirement are few.

---

[26] http://shawnroe.com/why-investing-beats-savings/

JAN: This is definitely something you should discuss with your prospective club Members before you agree to be in the club. While it's okay to have a healthy mix of risk tolerances among your Members, you want to be sure you're not setting up a fight every month. For example, if you're the only risk-averse person and everyone else has a high-risk tolerance, you're probably going to be a very unhappy camper who is uncomfortable with every purchase. You may even be the lone recurring "No" vote in the club. But even if that is the case, remember, you're paying $50 for the knowledge you're getting. You can always go back into your own portfolio and buy riskier things.

Q: Is this going to work?

JASON: Yes!

CHRIS: Yes!

JAN: It is! It's going to work. Not only is the club going to work, but you're going to invest money and you're going to make some money and you're going to lose some money, but overall, it's going to work.

Things to Remember

- An investment club is only as risky as you are. If $50 is a lot for you, then it is a bigger risk than if $50 is not a lot of money. If $50 is too risky, your club can decide on a lower amount for each Member to invest each month.
- Risk also comes from your manifesto and the investment style your club is interested in. Some clubs declare that they are comfortable with a higher degree of risk than others.
- It is a-ok to have a different investment style in your club than you do for your own personal savings or retirement. Our club was designed to be a learning lab, and some of our Members would never be as risky in their personal portfolios.

Homework

- Take a risk quiz! The internet has several available for you, like this one from Rutgers[27].
- If you have other investment accounts, look at how risky those investments are, and then you can decide how risky you are willing to be.

---

[27] http://njaes.rutgers.edu:8080/money/riskquiz/

- Write down the riskiest thing, outside of investments, you are willing to do. Now, go ask other people what is the riskiest thing they would do. Compare! It is fun to see how each of us is different regarding what we actually consider risk!

Chapter 8: Strategy

Your adrenaline is pumping. You're considering how much risk you are okay taking--both for the club and for yourself personally. Let's rein it in and talk strategy. Gotta direct that energy somewhere!

Q: Does the club have an investment strategy or philosophy?

JASON: Really, the investment strategy of our club is growth. That implies some risk. The investment strategy is built in to our stock analysis spreadsheet. We ask questions like, "Did the company's revenue double in the last five years?" and we input numbers from the S&P research report that help us answer them. This question, along with others, let us determine if we think the company will continue to grow. We don't pick a specific sector or type of company. Any stock, any company, is open for consideration as long as they are growing and we think they will grow our portfolio.

CHRIS: We have a club Manifesto which states our philosophy. Here it is:

> This is a "get rich SLOW" club. If we get rich faster, we're cool with that. But fast is not our promise.
>
> This is a learning lab. Your tuition is $50 a month. Take what you learn, go out into your "real life," and invest more on your own.
>
> We buy what we know, are interested in, like, and understand. We believe that this is the best starting place for building a solid portfolio. If we don't understand it, we don't buy it.
>
> We do not diversify our portfolio to reduce risk. We LIKE risk. Safe doesn't teach us what we want to learn.

We're really just trying to make money, and we're trying to learn from our mistakes. If you don't make mistakes, you're not going to learn anything. As a club, if we were really playing this safe, it wouldn't be fun and we wouldn't be making the kind of money that we're making today.

JAN: Your club should spend some time talking about your investment strategy or philosophy (like growth, value, or income for example) — even creating your own Manifesto — at the very beginning, maybe before you even decide to form the club and you're just having conversations with people, but definitely at your first meeting. You want to find out what people are comfortable with. It might make for very interesting club meetings if you have three people who are very conservative and four people who are very risky, but over time, it might cause issues if people aren't at least semi-aligned. It's one thing to have your own strict style and then give a little bit in the investment club. Again, this is a group decision; people are voting. It's majority rule, and it's a pool of money, not just "yours". As much as I have always hated "group work," I think that over time, groups of people make better decisions or do better work than individuals, especially in an environment like this. Certainly, I think the club makes better decisions than I would have made on my own just starting out.

CHRIS: Your club may have a philosophy and strategy on how it's going to purchase stocks, but that doesn't mean that it has to match your own personal strategy. Let's say the club is presenting four stocks at a meeting, everybody talks about them, and the club votes to buy one of those four but there was another one that you liked better — maybe it was lower risk, maybe it was higher risk. There's nothing that stops you from being able to change up your own investment style outside the club. Again, the goal is for you to learn what your tolerance is, what your preference is, what you are getting out of this and what you feel is right for you so that you can learn to do this on your own as well.

For example, I think my risk tolerance is probably higher than Jan's. On the buying side, we probably would both buy at the same time but, on the selling side, I tend to hold onto things (maybe a little bit too long in some cases), whereas Jan will sell things a little bit faster than I will.

Q: Does your club's investment strategy match your personal investment strategy?

JAN: Interestingly enough, when I rolled some money from a 401k into my SEP IRA, I let it sit there for a little bit while I really scoured our club portfolio and looked to see what had been our best-performing stocks. I had several criteria for what I wanted to buy. I knew I wanted to buy maybe four or five stocks that we had done well with, that I was familiar with, and that I knew. But I looked for more aggressive stocks—things that had doubled in the past three, four, or five years.

On the one hand, I was more conservative in that I looked at each stock's prior performance in our portfolio instead of just going rogue and trying out new things that were untested, as it were. But Chris is right: I do sell things more quickly, and I have made some trades in that portfolio to balance what I want the risk to be among those stocks. There are some things that I started out with that I thought were going to be great that I've since sold (I'm looking at YOU, Buffalo Wild Wings - BWLD), and then there are some things that I liked a lot and I bought more and more and more of every time I got a chance (Hello, Amazon - AMZN!).

I definitely do my own thing with my portfolio, and sometimes I have to remember that, even though the club might make a decision that I would not make, I can go into my own portfolio and make that decision my own way, so it's okay. I don't have to get all worked up about whether I like or don't like something that the club did. I can make my vote be heard and I can state my reason, and the vote goes the way it goes. Then I go into my own life, and I make the decisions that are going to impact me more directly.

Things to Remember
- It is good to come up with some guiding principles for your club so that every Member is aware of the purpose of the club and the overall investment strategy.
- Your club's investment strategy does not need to match your own personal investment strategy.

Homework
- Decide what investment strategy makes sense for your club.
- Create a manifesto for your club to make it easier to get all of your Members on the same page.

Chapter 9: Stock Picking

You're Manifesto'ed up, you've been thinking about strategy, and you want to know "When are we getting to questions about the stock picking part?" Well, here they are!

Q: What kinds of investments does your club make and why?

JAN: We just buy individual stocks. Right now, we don't do any mutual funds or funds of any kind, including index funds. We don't invest in bonds or anything else—just straight up stock market stocks for individual companies—mostly companies that we know, whose products we use, and that we reasonably understand or have an interest in.

CHRIS: That's a key point. We research stocks, and we have a methodology of evaluating a stock to see whether or not it's interesting to us. Most of the discussion we have around stocks is, "Do we understand what this company does? Does it make something we buy? Does it make something we use? Do they provide a service that any of us have ever heard of? Is there something specifically exciting about what this company is doing?" A lot of that is a judgment call based on those factors.

JAN: Some examples of that would be Amazon (AMZN) — I know, when we picked Amazon back in 2009, a lot of us were already big Amazon users — and companies like Disney (DIS); Estée Lauder (EL), which owns a lot of different makeup brands, not just their own; and also Constellation Brands (STZ), which has a lot of different beers, wines, and liquors. Those are all simple enough to understand. We do branch out occasionally, but those have been some of our better performing stocks. As of September 2016, our initial purchase of STZ was up 964%, and it's gone as high as 1000% — no joke!

Remember, too, that we started this club at the end of 2008 when "the economy was going to hell". So one of the questions we asked when looking at stocks in early 2009 was, "What products do well in a recession?" Chris researched this and found that alcohol and makeup are two of them, and those have been some of our best investments.

CHRIS: When we branched out and bought some stock in 3D printers and software that controlled 3D printers, none of us understood that at all, but we were excited about it because as part of the research, people said, "Well, this is what's happening within this space. These are some of the neat things that none of us have ever heard of that people are doing and developing."

Q: How do you decide what you buy? What do you look for in a stock?

JASON: Well, for your investment club, that will depend on your investment strategy. Since our strategy is long-term growth[28], we're looking at growth stocks, and we have a spreadsheet that will look at different financials for the company and see if they're a company that appears—at least on paper—that they will continue to grow and actually double in their size within the next five years.

Now, if we had a different investment strategy — if we were all closer to retirement age, for example — we may be looking for companies that pay good dividends or for companies that continue to maintain value even in up-and-down stock markets because that might be more of interest to us. But, right now, what we're looking at is growth stocks.

JAN: We also look at the news. What is the company getting ready to do? What most

---

[28] Don't worry if you don't understand all these terms at first reading. We didn't either. Use the Education portion of your club meetings to address a new term or topic each month. It's a learning lab--that's the design!

recently happened or is about to happen? You can get a lot of information from their quarterly reports or their annual reports, but there's also the future. So even if a stock looks pretty decent or maybe even just meh, sometimes we get excited about a company anyway because we know something that's happening in the future of that company, the way it's expanding, for example, or maybe a new market is opening up for some company and they're going into a new branch of business. We consider that as well. We look *beyond* the numbers in addition to looking *at* the numbers.

CHRIS: Every company has a story, and we like to hear what a company's story is and discuss how that's going to play into what they're doing and what they're going to do in the future.

JAN: Sometimes, this means we hold onto a stock longer than we should just because people are sentimental about it or they like the company or a product they make, but maybe it's not a great investment. So, although we have a strategy for dispassionately deciding what to sell, we just have to be aware that, sometimes, we can get attached to certain stocks, which is not always a good thing.

Q: As an investment club Member, what is it exactly that we're investing in? What am I getting for my $50?

CHRIS: You're actually investing in the club itself. You're buying a portion or a percentage of the investment club. And the investment club is what is investing in the individual shares of other companies.

JAN: You can look at it in two different ways: The club is purchasing shares of stock in certain companies, and then each Member—based on how long they've been in the club and how much money they have invested to date—then owns a certain number of shares, or a certain percentage, of the club's portfolio. If we have ten Members, for example, that doesn't mean that everybody has a tenth of every single thing. It depends on how much money you've actually put in. Think of it as taking the club portfolio slicing it up according to the amount of money you have put in, and you actually own that much of the club's portfolio.

CHRIS: Right. You don't personally own a share of Apple (AAPL); you own a share of the club's portfolio, which owns a share of Apple.

Q: So, how does one pick a stock?

CHRIS: I'll tell you how I do it. In the months before my turn to research and present a stock, I think about things that I'm interested in or places I've gone or things I've seen, and I try to find the companies that are associated with those things. Like, if I went to the movies and I saw a movie I really liked and that movie was packed — the way it happened when we bought Marvel — I would go online and see if Marvel is a publicly traded company. If they are, can we buy their stock? And then I'd conduct my research from there. Sometimes, I might find out that it's not really the company that I was initially interested in that's doing well. It might be another company--a competitor or a closely related company. We use the spreadsheet that Jason was talking about earlier.

JAN: When we sit down to fill out the spreadsheet, we use analysts' research — in most cases, the Standard & Poor (S&P)[29] report that we find on our E*TRADE account site — and we plug numbers into the spreadsheet. These numbers then answer 20 YES or NO questions that help us decide whether to buy the stock or

---

[29] The Standard & Poor report on E*TRADE has been rebranded as CFRA.

not. The number of YESes that we get helps us determine if the stock is worth further analysis or further research or if we should skip it based on the number of NO answers.

The questions our spreadsheet is configured to answer are below:

TEST
Did the Revenue DOUBLE in 5 years?
Did the Revenue CONTINUOUSLY increase?
Did EPS DOUBLE in 5 years?
Did EPS CONTINUOUSLY increase?
Did the company pay Dividends each year?
Did Dividends CONTINUOUSLY increase?
Current Operating Margin greater than 15?
Did Operating Margin CONTINUOUSLY increase?
Is Return on Equity greater than 15?
Are Current Assets greater than 2x Liabilities?
Are Quick Assets greater than Liabilities?
Is EPS growth predicted to be above 15?
Is Long Term Debt to Capitalization less than 33%?
Is Institutional Ownership greater than 40%?
Is Revenue growth Q/Q greater than 15%?
Is EPS growth Q/Q greater than 15%?
Did Sales grow 15% each year?
DID ROE/ROI CONTINUOUSLY grow over 5 years?
Is Current P/E ratio greater than 10?
Is the current price in the bottom third of 52 week range?
TOTAL NUMBER OF YES (out of 20)

CHRIS: After several years of doing this, we still gravitate towards the S&P reports. We like them because they have all of the information we like to see, and it is (almost) always in the same place in the report, which makes it easy. There are lots of different reports you could use (Thompson Reuters, Morningstar, etc.), and depending on which brokerage you select, you may have access to different reports.

Q: How do you know when to sell and what to sell?

JASON: You don't!

JAN: This has been the question that our club has dealt with for a long time, and for several years, whenever this conversation would come up, the prevailing thought was, "Well, even if we've lost money, we should just hold onto the stock because it may go back up," or "We've already sucked this cost, so let's just ride it out."

Sometimes, that has played out nicely. In the case of Bank of America (BAC), we lost a lot of our initial investment, and then it started gaining again. But, in a few other cases, the stock fell and just continued to fall.

At the end of our seventh year (2015), we decided that the most basic way to decide what to sell is look at the performance of the bottom of the portfolio. Now, every quarter, we look at the lowest-performing 10% of the stocks, and we put the club on notice. "These are the three (or four or five) stocks that are not doing well. Next month, at the end of the quarter, we're going to sell them. If, for some reason, you think we should hold onto this stock, then you should do the research and come back to the club next month with data that will convince us that we should keep it. If you don't do that—or if nobody does that — then the stock gets sold as a matter of course." We figured this was the most impartial and dispassionate way to do that. It takes the personal attachment out of it and still allows people to "dance for their life," as it were, on behalf of the stock. You can still argue to save it. If you don't, then that's fine too. That frees up money we can use to purchase other stocks.

Every time we sell a stock, there's a $6.95 transaction fee because that's what E*TRADE charges[30]. If we sell one stock, it costs us $6.95. If we sell five stocks, it costs us $6.95 times five. The intention is to minimize losses and look at the whole portfolio every quarter as opposed to once a year — or as opposed to never looking at it and just continuing to buy things. In the long run, that also helps keep the number of stocks more manageable because, at some point, you could have 40, 50, 60, even 70 stocks, and it's difficult for only twelve or fifteen people to keep track of what all those companies are doing. If we routinely get rid of the bottom 10%, the theory is that we will have a better performing and more manageable portfolio in the long term.

CHRIS: Two things that we realized: One is that

---

[30] E*TRADE charged $9.99 until March of 2017. Other brokerages charge different amounts per trade.

it's hard to manage 50, 60, 70 stocks, especially if you're doing well. On average, our portfolio is up—way, way up—so we didn't notice that some of our stocks were doing very poorly and had been doing poorly for a long time because their impact on our total portfolio was very small. (Remember, we typically only buy $500 worth of any one stock at a time, which means we have a lot of different stocks in our portfolio.) But if we had noticed it sooner and sold those stocks sooner, we would have had more money that we could have invested in things that were doing well. But because we just had so many stocks in our portfolio, we didn't pay attention. We just missed it, and that's something we're now actively trying to avoid. Now, each person in our club "owns" 3 or 4 stocks apiece, meaning those are the stocks they are responsible for keeping up with. Every three months (or more often if they want to), they report the news on that company. A quick Google search is all it takes if you don't read a regular paper or other business publication. We also advise each Member to set up a Google Alert on that stock so keeping up with the news on that stock is automatic. Google Alerts send out emails with news on anything you set them up to send.

The second thing is we've begun employing what a lot of companies use. When you're trying to get rid of dead weight or you're trying to figure out what's not performing well, you look at the bottom X% of your portfolio (or in the case of a company, the bottom X% of your employees or even your customers) and you just say, "Okay, that's what we're going to shed," and you don't get emotional about it. Just say, "It's not working for us. As long as the stocks we have are performing well and gaining value, we're fine. If not, we're getting rid of the bottom 10% every quarter." I think it's a good philosophy, and it ensures that you're doing a lot more research on new things.

JAN: It's also important to note that we came up with this approach and put it to the club, and the club agreed with that, so it's not just one or two people who decided that we were going to do this. The whole club agreed that we needed a strategy for selling, and after having fumbled around not having one, this seemed pretty simple, and everybody voted to adopt this approach. Of course, if the club sells a stock that you personally like, you can always buy it and keep it in your own portfolio.

CHRIS: Absolutely.

JASON: All the decisions that get made *about* the club are made *by* the club. For example, once someone does research on a stock and presents it to the club, the club will vote on it, and as long as we have a quorum, which for us is two-thirds of the club membership, a majority vote (of the

Members present) will decide whether we buy the stock or not.

Chris also made a very good point. Having too many stocks got really hard for us to manage, and so we really needed to trim them down. To be honest, I believe the whole 10% thing we're doing is very aggressive, but we need to be very aggressive right now with how large our portfolio has gotten. But I like what Chris said — as long as we have a certain number of stocks, we'll continue to do this because, eventually, if you just keep cutting off the bottom 10%, eventually you'll just be left with a handful of stocks.

JAN: To be clear, we vote to get rid of the lowest performing 10% of stocks we have held *more than a year*. We might buy a stock and it might not do very well over the next three months, but that doesn't mean we're going to then turn around and sell it after that short a time period. We're going to give it a year to prove its value and its worth in our portfolio, and then, after we have owned it at least a year, it could possibly fall into that bottom 10% being considered.

JASON: There's no real point in selling a stock *just because* it's in the bottom 10%. You really only want to sell a stock if you have something else to do with that money. You pay a transaction fee of $6.95 (or whatever your brokerage charges you) to buy it *and* to sell it, but even when there is only $250 or $300 sitting in the portfolio right now for that stock, there's lost money from our original investment. If you don't have anything to do with that $300, then there's really no point in selling it and just paying $6.95 and have it sitting in your cash accounts.

CHRIS: Exactly.

Q: What if we pick the wrong stock?

CHRIS: Sell it. That's kind of a flippant way of saying it, but the important part is that it was said without emotion. If you make a bad decision, you make a bad decision. You can't just sit there and be terrified of making another bad decision the next month. You've just got to keep soldiering on and keep going. You're going to make bad decisions. We've invested in companies that have ended up going bankrupt. It just happens.

JASON: The really good thing about being in an investment club is that we're getting more than just a share of a stock portfolio. We're getting education and experience. If we buy the wrong stock, we've each put in $50, or $500 total for that stock purchase. If that stock goes away or is no longer in our portfolio anymore, it was the wrong stock. Well, okay, we just need to take this as a learning experience.

Reviewing a stock's performance gives you the opportunity to take a look at how you chose that stock, what it was when you first researched it or considered it, and said, "Hey, this could do great!" and whether or not the initial decision was based on gut feeling or more of "Yeah, this has got a track record, and it has got the financials behind it." Both of those cases — gut feeling and track record — can either prove to be phenomenally awesome or not awesome at all. It just gives you another opportunity to continue to learn, to grow, and to improve your investment style.

Things to Remember
- An investment club can invest in any kind of tradeable security (stocks, bonds, futures, mutual funds, index funds, etc.).
- What you look at when purchasing a stock is a personal choice (and we have shown you what we find important and easy enough to figure out).
- You will make mistakes and pick the wrong stocks. You will also make smart decisions.

Homework

- Decide what your club is willing to invest in. For example, our club only invests in publicly traded individual company stocks. We do not invest in bonds or mutual funds.
- Review our list of 20 questions our spreadsheet answers when we are analyzing a company's financials. Can you think of some others?
- Quick! Write down the first 10 companies you can think of!
- Quicker! Look around where you are right now and write down 10 companies that make the things you see.
- Check with Google Finance[31] to see if it is possible to buy stocks in these companies.

---

[31] https://www.google.com/finance

Chapter 10: Teaching and Learning

That last chapter really got your gears going! You've probably discussed "strategy" with your investment club, and you're mulling over the mechanics of stock picking. Well, it's like riding a bike: You don't learn how to do it by READING about it. You have to actually GET ON THE BIKE—or in this case, dig into the research and start figuring out what makes a good stock (as far as you can tell). This is where the meaty part of learning comes in, and you can only learn by DOING. So let's get going on that already!

Q: So, who's going to teach me in this investment club?

CHRIS: You are!

JAN: You're probably thinking, "How can I teach myself? I don't know anything!" It's okay. You will all teach each other!

Occasionally, one of the Members of our club, Stocks & Bondage, will go take a class or attend a seminar or an online webinar about a particular topic and bring that information back to the club for discussion. For example, I went to Rice University's Glasscock School of Continuing Studies and took an eight-week course on Stock Market Investing Fundamentals, which was for my own edification, but I also brought that information back to the club, and it has helped us understand some terms and concepts[32].

Or one of our Members may be looking at the spreadsheet we use and say, "I don't really understand P/E. What does that mean? Price to earnings ratio? What is that?" And somebody will volunteer to look into it and prepare a basic presentation for the club, open the discussion, and then everybody will chime in with what they know or other questions they may have about it. That is one of the Vice President's jobs in our club—to manage the education program and to encourage people to seek out information and bring it back and educate the rest of us.

At first, a lot of people in the club think, "Well, I don't know anything, so I can't teach anything," but that's not true. We all are here to learn, and the way you learn is by just getting out there and digging into stuff and trying to figure things out or maybe consulting an expert and then coming

---

[32] Try Googling "personal development courses finances and investing" (without the quotes) to see what comes up online. Add the name of your city for more location-specific courses.

back with the information and discussing it. Again, we're not getting PhDs in Finance here; we just need to know enough to understand the basics and to make some investments, and over time, that information and that knowledge will grow.

Q: What are some of the best resources that you have found while starting your club?

CHRIS: Google. I mean, really, I can't stress enough how much Google is a huge asset and how underused it is when people are trying to learn stuff. It can show you how to read a Standard & Poor's report. It can give you information on companies. It can tell you about what different terms mean. Sometimes, if I don't understand a term, I'll Google it, and based on the first website I go to, I may not understand at all.

A lot of times, Wikipedia is so academic that it's hard to understand some of the concepts there. But I can go to some other resources and get a better one. So if you can Google it and get some good definitions from different places, you'll learn it better.

I would say that going to just one resource is a bad idea when you're trying to teach yourself a new concept.

JAN: Some other good resources are Yahoo! Finance[33] and Investopedia[34], and there's also a website called Learnvest[35] that I know has some additional resources. Investopedia even has a "Term of the Day" newsletter that will email you finance terms you can discuss with your club.

JASON: But let's be honest: We didn't find the best resources out there, hence, richonfifty.com.

JAN: Yes, and one of our intentions with Rich on Fifty is to help narrow down the field of all of the things that are available on the web because it can be overwhelming.

Q: What are some of the worst resources you found when starting your club?

JAN: I'm going to tell you right now that the book—which shall remain nameless—was, in my opinion, one of the worst resources. It was so boring and so long, and as soon as I started reading it, I thought, "I don't even want to have

---

[33] https://finance.yahoo.com/

[34] http://www.investopedia.com/

[35] https://www.learnvest.com/

a club anymore! I mean, this is just not fun. This looks like a bunch of boring stuff." You know, we have said there are some boring things that you have to get done—like the bylaws and electing officers and all that kind of thing—but we want to make investing itself actually fun. The whole purpose of Rich on Fifty is to make it accessible and to cut through the BS that's out there. So, yeah, that book is definitely one of the worst resources—at least for getting excited about starting a club.

JASON: But that's the official guide, Jan! (ha ha!)

JAN: It *is* the official guide, and you know, I'm sure that they have *officially* talked a lot of people *out* of starting an investment club.

I think another frustrating resource—at least for me, personally, dare I say it—is bivio because the webinars are really for high-level or deep-knowledge investors, and it has been intimidating or confusing to listen to them. I have just been lost and have not found them that helpful. But we *do* use them for club accounting, so that part of their site is very useful.

CHRIS: Most of the books on investments, for me, fall into two different categories. They are either written for the person who's going to be a day-trader or somebody who already has a firm knowledge of financial concepts to begin with and they're really talking about some advanced theory, or they were telling me that I needed to go into real estate. I mean, really, those are the two kinds of investment books I've read, and across the board, every single one I read was boring—every single one. They were just painful to get through. I mean, it's one of those books where you read thirty pages, and then you're like, "Wait, what did I just read?" and you have to go back again thirty pages to see, "Oh, yeah, this is the first thing I remember—it's from thirty pages ago," because it just was so bogged down in details and boringness.

JASON: One of the other resources that people sometimes look at is emails that they get. "Buy this stock. Buy that stock." Also, I used to get a number of unsolicited phone calls from "stock brokers" trying to sell me on a stock. I have never ever bought one of those stocks, but I have tracked a number of those stocks and have never ever seen one make money.

JAN: I think it's interesting to note here our opinion on Motley Fool[36] because I do like their style. They take a light-hearted approach to investing, and they certainly provide a lot of information. But on the whole, it can also be overwhelming because, again, there's so much information. How do you guys feel about

---

[36] https://www.fool.com/

Motley Fool? Have you used it? Do you have an opinion?

CHRIS: I have the same opinion of Motley Fool that I do with that other website, Seeking Alpha[37]. I think they're both well-written. You can get some good information there. But if you decide you're going to buy and get a good deal, by the time you've read the article and digested it, everybody else that gets the exact same newsletter is thinking the exact same thing. And now you're not getting as good of a deal as somebody else is.

For example, if I worked at Motley Fool and I bought stock in Coca-Cola (KO)—let's say I bought a hundred shares of Coca-Cola—and then I wrote on Motley Fool what an amazing stock Coca-Cola is, at the very end of the article or blog post, I might put, "I own stock in Coca-Cola," because you're required to do that to let them know that, and then I send it out to three million people or however many are on the list, and half of those people go out and buy stock in Coca-Cola, I just probably bumped the price of Coca-Cola up.

When I look at those things, I think, "Okay, what other companies are like the companies that they're talking about that might also have the

---

[37] https://seekingalpha.com/

same fundamentals and might also be interesting?" Because I feel, in those cases, I'm really just putting money in the hands of those writers and their own personal portfolios.

JASON: I actually love Motley Fool.

CHRIS: I like the writing style. I like the information. But I would never use their stock picks.

JAN: Tell us about that, Jason.

JASON: I subscribe to the Motley Fool Stock Advisor and have found a number of good companies to invest on based on their advice.

What I like about Motley Fool is that if you subscribe to that service, you get two picks a month, and they really go in-depth about the company. Some of them you can look at and say, "Well, I still don't understand what they do, and I would have no idea how to explain this to the group. I have no interest in buying this stock," and some of them are like, "Oh, my gosh, this is awesome!"

What the size of Motley Fool allows them to do is to interview CEOs and actually go into the companies and to see how well they're run because you can't always tell how well a company is run just based upon the general public information that's out there, and they do provide some of that. Motley Fool also has the same investment approach as us, buy good companies and hold them.

CHRIS: Jason, you mentioned something earlier that I think is worth repeating. You talked about how you got some unsolicited calls or emails from brokers who were trying to get you to buy certain stocks. For the first year-and-a-half or two years that we were in business as an investment club, every couple of months, somebody would show up with an email that they got that should have gone straight to spam that was talking about an amazing deal and the stock only cost $0.05 to buy and it was guaranteed to be well worth over $5 by the end of the year. To all of you reading this right now, don't be a sucker. Don't fall into those penny stocks. We try to only invest in the major stock exchanges like the New York Stock Exchange and the NASDAQ because, for those other ones, you can't get enough information on the companies to get a good deal.

JASON: Look, if you want to invest in penny stocks, go for it. But my take on that whole industry is that the only people who are consistently making money on the penny stocks are the companies that tell you to go buy this penny stock. They will buy into it at $0.03, go rush off and tell everyone to buy into it, "It's going to be well over $5." It will bump up the price to $0.05 and they'll sell it all, and they will have 67% increase right there in their investment. That is my take on that industry.

CHRIS: Agreed.

Q: What investment concepts seem to be the most difficult for people to grasp?

CHRIS: P/E ratio, to me, is the one that seems like we have to go over and over again. That and just how to read a Standard & Poor's report.

JAN: I agree, so we've provided you with a guide to this in the Your Club's First Year (appendix) section of our book!

JASON: The other thing that I think is the most difficult is that we're all looking for signs that say, "This stock will do well." Unfortunately, there's no one thing to look at. So people will say, "Yeah, but their P/E ratio is perfect and their sales are really strong! Their revenue is also really good. How come the stock is going down if these two things are going well?" The whole concept is there are multiple things that need to come together for a stock price to go up; it's not just one little thing.

JAN: Another thing that is difficult for people to grasp—or maybe they have an erroneous understanding of it—is that the price of the stock itself actually means something. What I mean by that is, when we analyze a stock, two of the things we look at are the 52-week low and the 52-week high. I know that there have been some people in our club who don't want to buy a stock if the current price is near the 52-week high. But that doesn't mean anything. That doesn't mean it's not going to go higher; it also doesn't mean it's not going to go lower. But I think people think, "Well, if it's been high and it's low now, it'll go back to that high so we should buy it if it's at the middle or lower end of its 52-week range." But that doesn't mean anything. You can't predict what a stock is going to do, so that piece alone is erroneous thinking.

The other thing is, we made what I think was a big mistake early on when we did not buy Apple stock when it was $125. (This was way before the stock split in 2014.). Our reasoning was, "Well, we only have $500 to invest at a time. If the stock is $125 a share, we can only buy four shares of it." That doesn't mean anything either because we did not buy Apple stock when it was $125 a share. We did finally decide we were being ridiculous when it was at $470 a share, and we did buy it then. And, yes, I think we only bought maybe two or three shares at the beginning. We had some extra money in the club, and we had not purchased stocks for a couple of months, so we had some extra cash on hand and we were able to buy five shares, spending almost $2,400 in the process on that one trade. But, even at $470 a share, it gained more than $230 per share at its high (reaching about $700), and then split[38] seven for one and came down to about $67 and it has gone way up since then.

So, the price of a single share of stock does not indicate anything as far as your investment club is concerned. If it's a company that you believe in and you can only buy one share of it, there's nothing wrong with buying only one share of it.

Symbol	Last Trade	Qty	Price Paid	Market Value
AAPL	$111.12	67	$85.72	$7,445.04
02/08/2012		35	$67.24	$3,889.20
07/14/2014		15	$95.86	$1,666.80
03/02/2015		5	$129.11	$555.60
10/08/2015		12	$108.90	$1,333.44

---

[38] Everyone gets excited when a stock splits, but it doesn't really "mean" anything for the average investor. When a stock "splits," you still own the same value, you just have more shares. For example, if you own a stock whose price is $100 a share and it splits **2-for-1**, you now have **two** $50 shares of stock **for** every **one** $100 share you had before the split (1 x $100 = 2 x $50). Same amount of money, more shares of stock (in this case, twice as many). We think a stock split has more power to psyche you out than anything else. It makes you feel like you got something, when you really got "nothing". For a more in-depth explanation of stock splits, check out this Investopedia link.
http://www.investopedia.com/ask/answers/113.asp

CHRIS: We said all of that to say you can understand each item and each term individually very well and not understand how they all relate to each other. Like, when Jan was talking about how we look at the price of a stock in relation to its 52-week high or low, it's not that that doesn't mean something or it does mean something. It does or doesn't in context and in relation to everything else. It might be near the 52-week high because the company is on a growth spurt so you'd want to pick it up then, but you'd want to look at other factors as well.

Think of it like baking a cake. I know what flour is, what sugar is, what vanilla is, what eggs are...I get the ingredients. I can explain it to you. I can watch a YouTube video showing me how flour is made. But I could not look at five cake recipes and tell you, based on the amounts of each ingredient, which one is going to make the best cake. Each pastry chef is going to tell you what they think the best is.

We're in our ninth year of this, and we're still learning, and we will continue to learn because there are just so many variables. And you'll always need to learn more. We intend that the more we learn, the better we will do.

JAN: And we haven't even gotten into learning about things like options and futures and short-selling and stop orders and all of these things, so we still have room to grow.

CHRIS: Exactly.

Things to Remember
- Always keep learning. The more time you, and your club, put into your own education, the better your portfolio will perform.
- There are great, good and terrible resources out there. Make sure you don't just pick the first definition or the first website you come to for all of your advice.

Homework
- Read this chapter again. Seriously. And take notes this time.
- Now go visit all of the links we mentioned and read at least one article on each of them. Some of them will sound like gibberish to begin with, but that's how you will build up your vocabulary!

Chapter 11: Participation

Wasn't it a RELIEF to find out you can teach yourself? If you were like us when you were thinking about starting your club, you searched the Internet, found all sorts of things that overwhelmed you, and you *almost* gave up. Until you found Rich on Fifty, that is! Now we're telling you it's okay to construct your own knowledge and that YOU CAN DO THIS! In fact, that's how you're going to retain it—by building it yourself. In this chapter, we dig into the time commitment and what participation *really* looks like.

Q: What kind of time commitment is this going to take? How much time?

CHRIS: Eight years.

JAN: Ha ha! Yes. Okay, well, let's break it down.

The actual meeting time is about two hours a month. Our club meets the first Sunday of every month, from noon to 2:00 pm. We don't always take the entire two hours, although, at the beginning of 2016 we did because we had a lot to cover and some new directions to go in, and then we got more adept at moving through the topics so meetings went faster. Then we added more Members, and now we own over 40 stocks, so there's a lot to keep up with. On average, our meetings last about an hour and a half now.

Then outside the club, Members do research. We ask each of our Members to do research at least twice during the year, so during two of our meetings each year, they present research. With 15 Members, for example, this means we'll have research presented at least 30 times throughout the year, which translates to 2-3 people presenting at least one stock each month (and many Members present more than one stock during their month). If you're taking time to do research, we suggest at least three hours for that outside of club time, and it can take longer. You might get lost in the process and really like it or you might do an hour here and an hour there, but it's not something you can do 30 minutes before the meeting and do it well and then pull out some report that you're going to use to now try and convince people to purchase this stock. It really does take more time than that.

I personally like to wait until closer to the end of the month to research a stock for the next meeting because I want to have the most up-to-date stock price information. The rest of the information about the stock, such as annual revenue, earnings per share by quarter or by year, etc. — those numbers don't change from week to week. No matter what month we're in when we're doing the research, the quarterly earnings reports are the same; they don't change except for when the new information comes out (quarterly or annually). But the current news and the current stock price are obviously different, and so I like to wait until closer to the meeting time to do my research, but not the day of the club (the first Sunday). I like to do it on a Friday or Saturday when I've got a couple of hours of uninterrupted time.

Then, outside of that, we have officers of the club who may have meetings or phone calls or who want to take time to look at the club's direction, review or choose the education topics, or do some other administrative things like that. Jason can speak to how much time the Treasurer's job takes.

JASON: The Treasurer's job takes about an hour to two a month, generally, and then there are the other things. The Treasurer audits the books and does the taxes[39]. You do that once a year[40].

---

[39] Our online accounting software program (bivio) takes care of this feature and generates the K1 statements each Member needs to file with his or her own personal tax documents.
[40] See Your Club's First Year for the full calendar of events, which includes these.

You could audit the books every quarter; that would make the one audit for the whole year a lot shorter, but that will take probably three to four hours, and that is simply just for the Treasurer.

JAN: And then, there is time the Secretary or other officers spend emailing club Members to remind them of the meeting time and date (which we still do after more than eight years!) or to share the portfolio results as of a certain date before the next meeting. That doesn't take very long — maybe twenty or thirty minutes.

We have a meeting each month for eleven months, and our last meeting of the year is a Christmas party. We may or may not discuss business, but we don't generally present research or do any other regular club activity at that time. Instead, we have a potluck dinner, we celebrate our successes, and we talk about the future.

JASON: And that "meeting" actually may be longer than two hours.

JAN: Yes, and we drink — most of us.

We also fantasize that "one day," we will have an annual meeting like Warren Buffet and Berkshire Hathaway, where we will have swag bags with goodies from all the companies we own, ha ha!

CHRIS: We just gave you the basics—the guidelines and "rules" we use to run our club. We have a very casual club. We make good money, but it's very casual. You could have a club that's a lot more active. If you wanted a club where you had people who were looking at stuff every day or you're doing votes by email over the course of a week, you could certainly do a lot more, and it would take more time. But the time that we've indicated here is really just to run a barebones, minimum, casual club that is still going to make some money and the Members are still going to learn some stuff. So it really runs the spectrum, I think.

JAN: I personally would not recommend meeting less often than once a month. I'm sure there are clubs that meet every other month or even once a quarter, but to me, that's not often enough. I think you have to meet monthly to keep up with what's going on. The more stocks we have, the more important it is to keep up with them every month. Outside of the club, I look at my own portfolio sometimes every day. Sometimes, I look at it two or three times a week, but a week does not go by without me looking at my own personal portfolio for at least thirty minutes to an hour over that week.

CHRIS: Agreed.

Q: How do you encourage club Members to remain involved?

CHRIS: As we said, we all take turns evaluating stocks. We do have the annual holiday party where we try to get some excitement built up, and in January, we try to set the tone for the entire year. But around summer, it gets harder to keep Members motivated because people are going on vacations or they've got kids and they're going to be out of town. You've just got to keep people mindful of their commitment to the club. I mean, we aren't the mafia or anything. Usually after you remind people once or twice of their commitments, they will get into the groove.

JAN: I also occasionally will send an article to the club on an investment topic I am interested in or maybe it's something that we just talked about recently or it's an article about a stock that we own. I'll post it on Facebook and tag people or I'll send it in an email. I don't know if people read it or not, but it's something that I do because I'm interested and I want other people to stay interested. It's by no means "required reading," but I'm sure—for people who do take time to skim it—that it's a way of being involved and keeping their hands in the business of the club in between meetings.

JASON: Also, as we said earlier, about a year

ago, we instituted a practice where we randomly assigned each stock we own to a club Member for them to "own." Every Member now has three stocks they will be responsible for, which means keeping up with the company's news, finding out when earnings reports are coming out and what they say, and then updating the club at least three times a year on the company so that we can continue to grow our portfolio — or in some cases to sell a stock based on new information.

JAN: I'm excited about this because now we can be alerted to the news and things that are happening more frequently than just once a quarter when we look at the low-performers. Our portfolio is fairly big right now. We have 42 stocks and 15 Members, but that's only 2-3 stocks each Member has to keep track of, so it's not difficult to do. Members can easily put a recurring appointment in their calendars to check the news on Amazon (AMZN) or see what's going on with Estée Lauder (EL), or they can set up a Google Alert to automatically receive information on a given company or topic, and then they can come back and present some information as part of the club's overall check-up. I'm thrilled that this is now part of our club's monthly agenda!

Q: How do you make investing interesting for people who are not at all interested in investing?

JASON: You make money.

JAN: I presume people are interested because they're in the club. But, within the club, there is a wide range of interest, and some people just do the bare minimum to get by, and they let the rest of the club carry them. Until we required everybody to do research twice annually, we went a year or two with some people never doing research at all. Some of us really like doing research, and we would do it often, but we want to hear from everybody, and we want everyone to learn. We don't want to make this a club of four with 15 Members; we want to make this a club of 15, and we want everybody to be involved. A lot of times, people don't do the research because they're scared of it, and they think they don't understand enough; they feel dumb. But that's the whole point of the club — you muddle through, and you come back and you say, "You know what? I tried to do this, I plugged in the numbers, but I don't understand this part," so then that's a teachable moment, and that's an opportunity for us to discuss something and learn, and it forces participation. But at the same time, we're not requiring some ungodly amount of homework every month that people are going to resent doing. We want this to be fun. It's a stretch, but it's a fun stretch.

Things to Remember
- You'll get out of this what you put into it. Although the time commitment isn't THAT much, it's the QUALITY of the time you put in that matters. When you're working on club business, be focused and intend that you learn something and that you also support others' learning.
- Being an officer in your club will significantly increase what you learn and get out of the club. Never been a leader? No worries. These are your friends, remember? They will support you as you learn to lead them. You can do it!

Homework
- Based on what your club has been discussing so far, find at least two articles related to companies that interest you and share them with your club between meetings. Ask a relevant question to get the discussion going via email, and follow

up on it when your club meets next month.
- Review the description of the officers' roles in Chapter 4: Operations, and make sure you (if you're an officer) are keeping up with the duties. Not every task will occur every month, but most will. Keep the description handy to remind you of what you promised your club, and report on what you've accomplished to keep yourself on track.

Chapter 12: The Impact

See? The time required to get your club started and to keep it going isn't all that scary! You CAN do this, and you can do it in the spare time you find here and there throughout the month. Even if you're an officer, you can fit this into your life—and what better thing to spend your time on than investing in your own knowledge and building your future income?

What ELSE will come of your investment? Read on to get motivated about the impact you'll have on yourself and others...

Q: How has being involved in an investment club changed your own investing activities?

JAN: It has made me get off my butt and actually *have* some investing activities. I'd always thought about it. I dabbled in it, but I'd always done less than I wanted to do, or I'd think, "Oh, someday I should do that" or "I really need to get it together" or "After I learn a bunch of stuff, then I'll invest."

Just having the club has made me buckle down

and get on the court in my own investing life. It had me start a Roth IRA or convert a regular IRA that I've had for a long time.

I also was very interested when I took a job for a two-year period with a company that had a 401k because I had been in public education prior to that, and I didn't have any opportunity for one before. As I said earlier, I put money into the Texas Teacher Retirement System (TRS), but I was not able to direct how that money was invested like you can to some extent with an 401K, so when I was able to invest in something I could at least sort of control, that was a great benefit. The company I worked for matched my contributions up to 6%, and I was able to direct where my money went within a group of funds. I was able to choose.

When I left that company, I rolled my money into a SEP IRA — a simplified employee pension individual retirement account — and I can invest in stocks or mutual funds or whatever.

So just having a club made me aware. It made me get on the court. It made me get into action, and when I would look at the club's portfolio, I would then think, "Well, let me see what my portfolio is doing," or "Let me see what the club did; maybe I want to buy some of that."

It's definitely upped my game a thousand

percent.

CHRIS: It did the same thing for me, too.

I dabbled in investing before, and I didn't really know what I was doing, so I kind of gave up doing it. I had a 401k at my company, and I didn't know if it was doing well or not doing well. I just did the "set it and forget it" thing. I bought into one fund in the 401k plan, and that was it. I just let them manage the whole thing.

Now that I've been in the investment club for over eight years, not only do I still have my 401k but I've got two other investment accounts that I invest in as well — one is for my mad money, and one is for supplemental retirement stuff. I look at that account every day just like Jan does. It becomes kind of like an addiction because I want to see how well I'm doing. It's like I'm kind of playing an investment game with myself and I feel much more confident doing that.

When I started getting confidence after being in the investment club, I was no longer happy with the performance of the investments people were making for me because I saw that we were doing so much better on our own than with these "experts" who were charging money to manage my money. It really transformed my entire way of thinking and what I do with my investments.

It also has a happy byproduct: It caused me to

take control of my own personal finances. Outside of the companies I was investing in, I was irritated that I didn't have more money to invest. I wanted to do more of it, and I looked at my own finances and I was like, "Why am I spending money doing this?" or "Why am I putting money into that?" or "Where am I wasting my money?"

It helped me run my life more like people run their businesses.

JAN: That is a great point because, sometimes, I look at a new pair of shoes and I think, "$150 for these shoes, or I could buy ten shares of XYZ stock!"

CHRIS: Yeah!

JAN: I really do, and you need to understand how much I love shoes! That has definitely changed my focus, and now, sometimes, when I have a surplus in my business account, instead of paying myself extra money directly, I think, "Oh, I could put $1,000 into my SEP IRA." And so, it's kind of like I sneak money away from myself and invest it instead of just blowing it on something or having a little bit more to spend that week or that month.

CHRIS: Here's something else it's done for me. My mom recently retired, and she doesn't know really anything about investing or finances. Her entire career, she was required to put money into the Teacher Retirement System (TRS) here in the state of Texas (instead of Social Security, which Texas teachers are not eligible for). She also had a financial advisor who invested her other money, but she didn't know where it was, what it was invested in, and if it was doing well or not doing well.

She started getting letters in the mail from these companies telling her she had some kind of action on her account and her financial planner has now retired—he's not taking calls anymore. What being involved in this investment club has given me is the confidence and the knowledge to take my mom's retirement accounts and understand what's going on with them and be able to help her maintain her standard of living through retirement, figure out what to do with this money now that she is retired and make some smart choices for her.

JAN: That's great.

CHRIS: Yeah, I love that.

JASON: Your answers sound awesome, and I wish I had done all that, but I bought some stocks before the club. How I picked stocks was more like throwing a dart at a dart board. But then, that was really kind of like a savings account. And then I sold all the stocks and bought something with it, and that's all I've done on the personal side. I'm still a "set it and forget it" kind of guy on my 401k, but now I'm kind of inspired. I really need to take charge of that and maybe I'll get to work on my own personal finances as well.

CHRIS: Well, Jason, I would also assert that you decided to help us write this book on Rich on Fifty. You've accumulated some kind of knowledge, and you see that there's a gaping void in this investment world and that's what you're going to contribute to. I'm inspired by that, too.

JASON: All right, there we go.

Q: How has the club changed over the years?

JASON: We've gotten better-looking.

CHRIS: Like a fine wine.

JAN: All true. And one of the *other* ways that we've obviously changed is we have changed in Membership. The original twelve or fourteen people who started the club are not all still here in our ninth year. I would say about six of us are, and the rest are people who have come in at various times. About a year and a half ago, we added three more Members and then a few more about six months ago. I think it's interesting that we don't actively recruit people now. I mean, we have since the very beginning, but people know that we have an investment club and they will say, "Tell me more about that" or "Are you taking new Members?" As I've said before, sometimes, there are people we think are a good fit who we know are going to do the research and stay involved and stay motivated, and we want them to be in our club, and there are some people who don't.

Another way, as we mentioned, is now our club is actively selling things that aren't doing well.

CHRIS: We've also become much more organized. I hate to say that it took us eight years to get organized, but it really has. Sometimes, you have to do something fifty times before you get tired and say, "There's got to be a better way," and you figure it out. It's the frustration of a lot of the things we've gone through over the past nine years that you're going to benefit from as a reader of Rich on Fifty because you're going to have all of our frustration worked out already, and you won't have to go through that. You're welcome.

Things to Remember
- You learn by DOING. The very act of investing and putting your attention on your money and your future will move you forward.
- You may be starting small, but you have STARTED! That's HUGE! Give yourself some props for getting this going. Soon, you will look back on your success and be astonished at how far you've come!

Homework
- Interview at least two people in your life who have investments of any kind. Ask them something you'd like to learn from them, such as "How do you choose what to buy?" or "How long have you been investing in stocks?" and really engage in the discussion with them. Be curious and respectful. Everyone has something to teach (and to learn).
- Write a few sentences about where you'd like to see your club in one year, five years, and ten years. Sure, it's a pie-in-the-sky dream right now, but it helps to have a target to shoot for.
- **BONUS POINTS**: Bring up this type of long-term planning/dreaming with your club Members at the next meeting. Make it an agenda item at least once per year to

keep the momentum—and the dreaming—going.

Chapter 13: Hindsight

You may have skipped straight to this chapter to learn from our mistakes first, and that's fine with us. But we hope you've read everything else since we spill the beans in every single chapter, not just this one. This part's short, thank goodness, since we feel it's all been a learning experience, but what good "how to" book would be complete without a "how NOT to" chapter? Exactly!

Q: What's the one thing that you wish you had done when setting up the club that you did not do?

CHRIS: I didn't spend enough time really looking at what it meant to be in an investment club, and it wasn't until after our first year that I really got what it meant. I mean, I knew *conceptually* what we were doing. I knew that I wanted to learn more about investing. But I wish I had spent the time or had been able to find a resource that really explained to me what it was I was doing, what impact it was going to bring to my life, and just how much better I was going to be at doing the investment thing. Without this club and my ongoing involvement in it, I would never have started my own investment accounts and spent the amount of time I am spending now on my own finances. I would never have started subscribing to *The New York Times* or *Wall Street Journal*. I really feel like I know a lot more now about the world around me than I did before.

JASON: Yeah, we should have spent more time on the education pieces at the start and continued that throughout the year. The club is set up so that you really should be learning something new every month. I think, if we had done that, we could have gotten better returns some years than we did, and I think we could have been more successful much earlier.

JAN: We've solved that for you with Your Club's First Year, so please do read that section and spend time digging in and adapting it for your own club's purposes.

CHRIS: I also wish we had done more with accountability and integrity. We do a great job with that now in the club, but in the early years, we were still really struggling with, "Are we doing this right?" "Is this wrong?" Back then when people would present education topics, sometimes, it would be like, "Well, I just printed out this Wikipedia article for us all to read," and we never really said that's not what we intend, and we never really guided people into doing a better job.

Now when we do an educational presentation, people really understand. You can tell when they get to the meeting that they've done the work to present the education topic, and people leave having really learned it.

The same thing goes for when people are presenting stocks. Some people would research one stock and say, "Here's the stock I researched and it's a terrible buy," and they would stop there. But even if you don't recommend it, we need to learn, "*Why* is this a bad buy?" We need to learn from the things that we're *not* buying, but we also are trying to make money, so don't stop at the one bad stock. Keep going until you find at least one thing that you would like to recommend the club purchase because we need to learn from both. I'm glad we're doing that now, but I wish we had put a little more effort into doing that upfront.

JAN: I also think that we should have talked about and maybe set some rules in place for when to sell a *high-performing* stock because, as I heard somebody say today, "You don't own the gains. You're just renting the gains until you sell." So, while we have, on paper, made quite a bit of money on a particular stock—I'm thinking about Netflix (NFLX), for example—we didn't always pay enough attention to it on a regular basis. That stock, when we owned it, gained and then lost a lot of value (2011), and maybe we should have sold at a certain point and taken those proceeds and then done something else with them.

We have not been good at selling stocks that do well — mostly because who wants to, you know? In some cases, there's no reason to, but I think we should have talked about that more up front. I think that's something that you just kind of have to figure out as you go. It probably was not something we could have done when we set this up because we didn't have enough knowledge, but it is something that I wish we had done earlier — to talk about when to sell.

CHRIS: I agree, and I think there's an attachment to particular stocks that we've alluded to in lots of different chapters of this book. There's this attachment that we feel, and it's almost as if people believe that, once you buy a stock and then sell it, you're done, and you can never buy that stock again.

It's kind of like that with a car, right? If I buy a new car and I like it and then I later sell it, I can't just go buy it back again, and so I'm stuck. Stocks aren't like that.

If something is high and you make a lot of money from it but you think it's going to start going down or you think it's peaked, you can sell it high and then wait for it to go back down and then buy it again and wait for it to go back up again. You can ride those waves if you want to. That's something that we don't think about often. It's a hard concept, for people to really wrap their heads around.

JAN: The other thing that I wish we had done earlier when we were setting up—at least after the first three or four months when people got more comfortable or at least understood how to use the spreadsheet to pick stocks—I wish we had assigned people to do research earlier rather than just letting interested people step up to volunteer. Several people in our club went six, eight, ten, even twelve months or more without doing any research, and I think it does a disservice to club Members. They get to hide out and not learn from their own work. But I think that's why people are there. They're in the club because they want to be made to learn. "This is the structure that we've put in place and I've agreed. Yes, I will be a participant."

And agreeing to participate and then just showing up and not actually doing any research or taking any action to help educate yourself or other people doesn't serve the purpose of the club, so I wish we had done that earlier.

Q: If you had to do it all over again, what would you have done differently?

JASON: Do not sell TESLA.

JAN: And I wish we'd bought Chipotle (CMG) back in 2008 or 2009.

Things to Remember
- Hindsight is 20/20, as they say. You WILL look back and wish you'd done a few things differently. It's okay. It's called wisdom.

Homework
- Stephen Covey says to "Begin with the end in mind." Building on the homework from the last chapter, think about where you'd LIKE to be in one, five, and ten years, and discuss with your club the actions it will take to get there. What will you need from your club Members? What kind of club will you have to be to get where you want to go? How can each Member be responsible for helping the club get there? It's not just the officers' job!

- Review Your Club's First Year and make some tweaks now that you've been meeting for a while. Don't be afraid to make our road map your own. Veer slightly off the path we've set, or blaze an entirely new trail. This is YOUR club. OWN IT.

Chapter 14: Reflection

This is the "orchids and onions" chapter where we tell you what we did well and where we fell on our faces. Fortunately, no one in our club is sensitive about the flubs, though we DO like to mention our wins quite a bit. The truth is, many of our successes were lucky stumbles, but they were grounded in our quest to buy companies that we know and understand, so there was *some* method to our madness. On the other hand, some of the things we ended up losing money on started out as good picks we just didn't pay attention to over the long haul. Your club will have some of each of these. Don't worry--it's the skinned knees of learning to ride the investment bike. You will learn, and you will heal!

Q: What are some of your major investing successes?

JAN: I'll just tell about a few of our top overall investments, and several of these we have purchased more than once.

Let's take our star performer: Constellation Brands (STZ). Overall, that stock is up 462%

since we originally purchased it in August 2009[41]. We also bought it again in 2012 and then twice in 2013. The lowest increase in that stock (as you can see from the 11/04/2013 purchase, our most recent for this particular company's stock) is 155.85% percent, so we've done very, very well. And our original purchase is up 1,028.54%. That's incredible! That's between 2009 to 2016. Over 1,028% — that's crazy! We paid $14.78 a share for that stock originally, and it's now $171.24. I'm not going to bore you with that for all of our whole portfolio, but that is an incredible success.

Symbol	Last Trade	Qty	Price Paid	Market Value
STZ	171.24	66	$ 29.81	$ 11,301.84
08/27/2009		33	$ 14.78	$ 5,650.92
08/07/2012		16	$ 29.89	$ 2,739.84
06/10/2013		9	$ 52.90	$ 1,541.16
11/04/2013		8	$ 65.68	$ 1,369.92

The way we found it back in 2009 was when Chris asked himself, "What products traditionally do well in a recession?" The answer: Alcohol and makeup. So Robert, being the consummate party thrower, volunteered to research alcohol, and he brought us STZ.

In this same vein, another stock we have done

---

[41] Information for STZ as noted in the graphic was current as of 10/10/2016.

very well with is Estée Lauder (EL). We're up 399.35% on our original purchase in June 2009[42]. Disney (DIS) we've bought three times now. Our original purchase is up 262.65% and overall up 137.74%. We've also done very well with Amazon (AMZN), and I personally own Amazon. In fact, a very large share of my portfolio is Amazon. Our original purchase in February 2011 is up 357.58% from a purchase price of $182.52. Today it is $841.71 a share.

Altogether, we have seven stocks that have increased more than 100% in value since our initial purchase of them, and we have another eight that have increased 20% – 95%, so those are some of our best successes.

CHRIS: We've also had some fun things happen, too. We decided to buy shares of Marvel when Marvel was its own company. The day after we purchased Marvel, Marvel announced it was being purchased by Disney. That's part of what happened with our increase in Disney. We got a great deal when we invested in that stock.

JAN: That was one of Chris's picks. I remember feeling like I was some sort of insider when that happened—like I really *knew* something, ha ha!

---

[42] Info for all stocks mentioned in this response was current as of 10/10/2016.

Q: What are some of your worst picks?

JASON: I haven't had any bad picks so I can't answer any of that.

JAN: Ha ha! Let's talk about what are *emotionally* bad picks. I mean, I'll talk about the statistics too but, emotionally, we had some rough patches over Bank of America (BAC) and Fannie Mae (FNMA), for sure.

CHRIS: Yeah, during the financial crisis was probably not the best time to purchase financial stocks, but we did. Bank of America has recovered; Fannie Mae has not.

JAN: We don't own Fannie Mae anymore, but we do still own Bank of America. It's way up now.

CHRIS: For me, our worst pick was probably JCPenney (JCP), and I hate to say that, but we invested in JCPenney because we believed in the vision of the brand-new CEO, Ron Johnson, who was previously in-charge of retail for Apple. We loved what he did. We loved his plans; we thought they were great. But the shoppers at JCPenney were perhaps not the same kind of shoppers that shop at the Apple Store, because the things that he was trying to implement should have made a much better shopping experience, but ended up rejected by their clientele.

JAN: But they wanted their coupons!

CHRIS: Yeah, they wanted coupons. They wanted fake discounts. They wanted to think they were getting great deals instead of just always getting the best price. It just didn't work out the way that he envisioned, and I'm really disappointed in America—really—for the failure of that JCPenney stock because I think he really had a great vision for a great company.

JAN: And it was a reasonable $32.40 when we bought it and we thought, "There's nowhere to go but up! They have all this real estate. They own all these stores. They have the brand recognition. They have a new merchandising person coming in. It's going to be fantastic." It was at $6.79 when we finally sold it. And lately, so many retailers have been closing their brick and mortar stores.

Our worst performing stock is ECOtality. We bought that stock and it was only $1.93—which, you know, that's almost like a penny stock, you would think—but with ECOtality we thought, "Hey, we're really getting in on the beginning of something." They build the charging stations for electric vehicles. You know, with our purchase of TESLA and some other information that we had, we thought, "This is where the future is. This is where it's going." Then, that company filed bankruptcy, and now our stock is worth zero. We lost 100% on that stock. It's been completely wiped out, and it still sits in our portfolio at $0 as a reminder.

Another stock that we had that did not do well over time is Quantum Fuel Systems (QTWW). We lost 86.5% on that (and they have since gone bankrupt). And then, disappointingly, Twitter (TWTR) and Pandora (P) both went down about 74% from where we bought them. We had a couple of 3D stocks that we loved, loved, loved—3D (DDD), Stratasys (SSYS) and Organovo (ONVO)—and they fell over 60%. That broke our collective hearts.

CHRIS: What's sad about some of those stocks is we held them when they were worth a whole lot more money. We made a ton of money (on paper) on those 3D stocks, but we just weren't paying attention to them over time. When we should have sold them, and retained our gains, we didn't. We thought that they would definitely bounce back, and they didn't.

JAN: An example of a stock that we know and use and understand is Michael Kors (KORS), and I thought Michael Kors was a great buy. I mean, I use his products. I buy his purses and shoes. He's in lots of stores, and he has his own stores.

We just bought that stock two years ago, and it fell and never recovered, so we axed it. Personally, I don't buy fashion stocks any more. People are too fickle. Tastes change.

Another emotional pick was Lululemon (LULU). We did really well with that for a while and then it lost money. The company made a couple of bad decisions in merchandising. They picked some fabric that was too sheer for their yoga pants, and it was a big scandal and a big problem. The way the company handled that wasn't so good, and so their stock is actually down just a little bit. We did hold onto it. It was down over 20% at one point, and we rode it back up. It's still down from where we bought it, but it has come back. We originally purchased it in 2011, and the original purchase is up 17.38% but then we bought it again in 2012 and that purchase is down 17.43%, so overall, we are down on Lululemon. But club Members resisted my snarky attempts to sell that stock multiple times, so we still have it.

Q: What's been the biggest obstacle to starting and/or running an investment club?

Jan: The first biggest obstacle was just getting started and figuring out what we needed to do since there was not such an easy-to-understand website out there like Rich on Fifty that is walking you through what to do and what not to do.

We're busy people. We don't have time to read 400 pages of a book on investment clubs that may or may not fit our strategy. We want the highlights. We want the DOs and DON'Ts. We want some templates. We want to just get it going.

Another one of the frustrating things at the beginning was it took us several months before we were ready to buy stocks, and that's the whole appeal of being in an investment club — starting a club and buying stocks! Finding out that we had to set up a lot of things at the beginning was a little disheartening to a lot of our people. Once we got going, we were fine, but that was an initial obstacle to starting it.

An obstacle that was an issue — I'd say in the early middle years — was people's participation. Back then our meetings were from 4:00 to 6:00 pm on the first Sundays of each month. At noon, I would start getting emails with all these people saying, "Oh, I can't come to the meeting." "I'm not going to be there." "I can't come this time. Have a great meeting!" Well, that impacts what the club can do as far as conducting business, as we said, because if we don't have quorum, we can't vote. And if we can't vote, we can't buy or sell anything.

And sometimes people *wouldn't even tell us* that they weren't coming. Fortunately, we have a pretty good group of people who at least communicate, but *communicating* that you're not coming and *not coming* have the same impact because we can't do business a third of our people aren't there. The smaller the club, the worse that is because each person's absence makes a bigger statistical difference. If you've only got five people in your club, and two of them can't be there, you can't do any business. This is one reason we advocate for you to have at least 10 Members if you can.

For a while, I got really disheartened about people's participation. I thought, "You're in this club, you signed up for it, and you're putting your money in. You should show up and participate." We understand that people travel for work. We understand that there are emergencies, but that's not the point.

The point is don't call us two hours before the meeting and say you can't come unless there's truly some emergency because it's only once a month. This is not something that you have to do Monday through Friday. And you know in advance what the dates are. It's the first Sunday of every month—and it's been that way for more than eight years. So attendance was an obstacle in the early middle years, but it's not so much an obstacle now, and I think the reason it's not now is that we have improved the ways we engage our Members. We have improved our educational component for sure. That being said, stay vigilant for signs that your club's attendance is flagging, and tighten it up before it gets to be a problem.

CHRIS: There's a very valuable lesson to be learned in all that, and it's that our club has these problems. Your club is going to have these problems or others like them, and there's nothing wrong with that. You're going to have these hiccups. You're going to have to figure out what works for you and what doesn't work for you, what your personal pet peeves are and what they're not. The group of folks we have now has pretty deep integrity, and I think that's what's making this work for us. We all know what the goal is. We're all on board with doing it, and we're just making it happen.

Q: What's the most important or surprising thing that you have learned so far?

CHRIS: Some people don't care about their money.

JAN: Yes.

CHRIS: That just really surprised the hell out of me, to be honest. Some people just don't care. Like, they're giving us $50 a month. This doesn't apply to any Members that we have today so much, but for some people, it was a purely social thing, and they didn't really care what we did with the money. I mean, I would love to have more people like that in my life who would just give me $50 a month. But in the context of the club, it really just shocked me.

JAN: The most important thing that gets reinforced for me month after month and year after year, and it's something that I knew but it continues to impress me, is how much money we can amass in a relatively short amount of time. Yes, it's $50 a month. Yes, we've had different numbers of people in the club as Members. But today, we have over $62,000 in our portfolio! None of us could have done that by ourselves at that rate, and I would not have learned as much had we not done this drip by drip, $50 at a time, every month for more than eight years. More than 100 months, as of this book's publication date. That has been impressive to me.

I can look at all the charts in the world that say, "If you put away 10% of your income when you start working at 22 years of age, you'll have $72 kajillion dollars when you retire at 65." But that knowledge doesn't make any difference. What makes a difference is seeing the portfolio grow and seeing the returns over time and seeing my teeny tiny $50 per month turn into $7,000 or $8,000 over the years. That continues to please me and excite me about the club.

CHRIS: One of the things that is important to think about too is we've had some phenomenal returns. As an individual, I would not have ever had those same returns with just my own investment. In the club, we're putting in $50 a month, but we're *all* putting in $50 a month, so we've got a lot more money to buy stocks with.

We've made good decisions. We've been able to put more money into those good decisions, so we've made more money from those good decisions, and I love seeing how that happens. While my own personal portfolio is doing well, my club portfolio is doing a whole lot better, and I love that.

JASON: Yeah, for me, it never would have come up to buy Estée Lauder (EL) or probably Constellation Brands (STZ) — two companies that have done very well for us.

JAN: And I certainly would never have bought Under Armour (UA).

CHRIS: I didn't even know they were a public

company until Jason brought them up.

JAN: Right, and we're up over 31% on Under Armour, and our original purchase is up over 83%. Good job, Jason!

Q: What are three concrete pieces of advice that you would give to people who are thinking about starting an investment club of their own?

CHRIS: Do it.

JASON: Do it.

JAN: Do it.

CHRIS: Oh, my god, there's our three pieces of advice right there!

JASON: Join richonfifty.com.

JAN: Yeah, just start. Figure it out. It's okay to be stupid. It's okay to not know. It's okay to ask dumb questions. Don't worry about that. Just get the people on the same bus going the same direction, and I promise you will get to a better destination over time. You're going to do better together than you would probably do on your own. I've always hated group work, but this is a place where group work makes sense, and the group does better work than I can do by myself. It makes me investigate and learn things I might be too lazy or too overwhelmed to look into on my own. When it's my turn to present an educational topic or a stock, I *have* to figure it out so I have something intelligent to say and something of value to present.

CHRIS: And don't be afraid. You're going to make mistakes, and it's okay. It's only $50 a month.

JAN: That's right. And ask questions. We are here at Rich on Fifty to answer them to the best of our ability, but ask other financial professionals, too. Read the news, pay attention, ask questions. Be interested. Participate.

And don't quit.

Things to Remember
- You will pick stocks that do astoundingly well, and you will pick some total duds. It happens. If everyone always picked winners, there would be no learning. It doesn't mean you suck or that you shouldn't have an investment club, so resist the temptation to "go there" or to

blame any of your Members who pick bad stocks. None of us has a crystal ball.
- It's a numbers game. The more stocks you research, the more good ones you'll find, and the better you will do over time. We promise.

Homework
- Be brave and discuss with your club some potential obstacles you see to getting Rich on Fifty. You may not actually be EXPERIENCING these obstacles now, but that doesn't mean you shouldn't speculate and discuss.
- **BONUS POINTS:** Tell your club where you're likely to drift away, what it looks like when you "get lazy," or what you're afraid will happen (ex: "Even though I'm into it NOW, I'm afraid I'll lose interest in the club and get bored.") Ask a friend to be an accountability partner to help keep each other on track, or use the club meetings to make a promise about what you're going to learn or accomplish in the coming month, then come back to the next meeting and report on how you did.

Chapter 15: The Future

Q: Here it is. Here's the ultimate finishing question. Where would you like to see your own club be in the next five years?

JASON: Jan, Chris, and I have been the leaders of this club pretty much since it started—for almost nine years. I don't know where I want to see it in five years, but within two years, I want none of us to be on the leadership team of this club, and we are already making that transition. I really think we've got a good group, and our Members could take us to places that we don't even know.

CHRIS: I agree. It always helps when you've got new people running things and Members taking turns running things because you get different opinions, different methods. I would love to see more participation on the leadership side as well.

JAN: I would like to see, in the next two years, all of our portfolio being stocks that are doing well. When I say "well," it means in the green. They don't have to be doing 10% or 12% or 100%

or whatever; they just have to be doing well. I really want to cut the dead weight, and I want to continue to do that. Obviously, we probably won't be able to maintain that forever going forward, but the greener, the better.

I second Jason's leadership call. I would love to be able to think I can walk away from this club and it would continue and even get stronger. I would also like to see people start new clubs. I have been asked to give some advice to a friend of mine who wants to be in our club. We don't have space right now as we're at our Membership limit, but I told her that I would be happy to talk with her friends and help them get an investment club started. If anybody in our club has the interest in helping other clubs get started outside of this Rich on Fifty initiative, I think that would be a great testament to it also — to go personally plant that seed and help nurture a club from the beginning so that you can guide a club to do things better than we did, which of course, is the intention that we are pushing out here through Rich on Fifty.

CHRIS: I would like to see our portfolio grow. I would like to see if we can maintain this level of growth.

JAN: Right now, our portfolio is up over 61% overall.

CHRIS: I mean, that's just incredible growth. That just blows my mind and I would love maintain that and I would love to see if we could beat it.

JAN: Yes!

Things to Remember
- Every club has a different strategy and picks different stocks. It's all good. Your club's strategy isn't "right" or "wrong". If, over time, your Members feel it's not working for you, then change it up.
- You're at the end of this book but NOT the end of your road. You're just getting started, and we are so thrilled for you! Please keep in touch with us, and let us know how you're doing. Got questions? We'd love to hear those as well, and we'll do our best to answer. Contact us at the Rich on Fifty website at any time.

Homework
- Compare your club's performance to at least two different indexes (for example, the S&P 500 and the Dow Jones Industrial Average). Don't know how to do this? PERFECT! Here's your next educational

piece to research and present to your club. We know you're smart and can figure this out, so go do it! (HINT: If you're using E*TRADE, it's on the PERFORMANCE AND VALUE tab.)

Conclusion

Congratulations! You've reached the END of the book, but the BEGINNING of your journey. You're well on your way to getting RICH ON FIFTY, and the work you do is going to change the financial trajectory of YOUR life as well as that of EVERY MEMBER in your club. That's HUGE, and YOU'RE AMAZING!

We want to end by saying a heartfelt THANK YOU!

THANK YOU for buying and reading our book.

THANK YOU for the time and attention you have given it and us and all of our ideas.

THANK YOU for the impact you are making on your current and future family.

THANK YOU for the contribution you are being to each Member, and

THANK YOU for the ripple effect you are helping our work have on the world at large.

We really appreciate you, and we are here to support you as you grow this thing even

BIGGER than you thought possible.

Finally, **please follow us on Facebook**[43] and stay in touch with us through **richonfifty.com**. We want to hear how it's going and what you and your club are creating. We want to hear your questions and provide you with answers, and we want to be an ongoing resource for you and your club. Remember, WE DID THIS, AND YOU CAN TOO!

Richly,

Jan, Chris, and Jason

---

[43] https://www.facebook.com/richonfifty/

Your Club's First Year

To make this even easier for you, we've prepared a detailed outline for a full year of club operations. (For a downloadable version[44]). Modify this as you wish, or use it exactly as presented; some people may speed through the entire year in three months, other people may need more time to get the club set up and not start with education until later. However you do it, be sure and let us know how it goes and what works and doesn't work. Drop us a line at the **Rich on Fifty** website. We'll update this in future editions based on your feedback.

MONTH	CLUB BUSINESS	EDUCATION	HOMEWORK /OTHER
Jan	Finalize meeting day/time/location/ refreshments Finalize amount each Member will invest per month	All of the topics in "Club Business" are education enough for this month! Look to the homework to keep the momentum going. Below, we	Research online brokerage accounts and compare. Come to the February meeting with suggestions. Research templates for

---

[44] https://www.richonfifty.com/resources/first-year-outline/

MONTH	CLUB BUSINESS	EDUCATION	HOMEWORK / OTHER
	Discuss risk level/comfort

Choose a club name

Review online brokerages

Review officer positions and responsibilities | suggest Education topics for you in future months, but always feel free to go with the direction your club is headed. If you have other interests, by all means, pursue them! | investment club bylaws to create your own draft. Your club will review, edit, and approve the draft at the next meeting. |
| Feb | Elect officers

Finalize initial Member roster

Choose your online brokerage firm

Review draft of club bylaws | Bylaws usually take a long time to go through, so this month we just recommend going through club business. | Treasurer sets up online brokerage account.

Each Member sets up online investment "bill pay" before March meeting.

Treasurer sets up club accounting software.

Officers prep for next meeting. (See |

MONTH	CLUB BUSINESS	EDUCATION	HOMEWORK /OTHER
			Chapter 5: "Running a Meeting".) Check out online resources for investment info and research (getting your feet wet). Begin making a list of companies you like and are interested in.
Mar	Choose investment style Begin a general discussion of what companies are interesting and might be worth researching	Common Investment Styles Stock research reports: What's in them?	Practice researching and analyzing a stock.

MONTH	CLUB BUSINESS	EDUCATION	HOMEWORK / OTHER
	Complete/approve bylaws Club agreement about research (how often, expectations, etc.) Signing up for research (each Member chooses 1-2 months, ex.) Review Member deposits; make sure all are scheduled Begin discussing companies Members like		
Apr	Practice researching stocks	**Looking at Basics:** Stock price Sales/Revenue	Selected Members do research for next meeting.
May	First stock research	**Looking at Basics:**	Selected Members do

MONTH	CLUB BUSINESS	EDUCATION	HOMEWORK /OTHER
	presented Vote on stocks presented	EPS Dividends	research for next meeting.
Jun	Follow club agenda outline	**Looking at Basics:** P/E Ratio Return on Equity	Selected Members do research for next meeting.
Jul	Follow club agenda outline	**Looking at Basics:** Liabilities Cash	Selected Members do research for next meeting.
Aug	Follow club agenda outline	**Looking at Basics:** Operating Income Assets	Selected Members do research for next meeting.
Sep	Follow club agenda outline	**Looking at Basics:** EPS predictions	Selected Members do research for next meeting.
Oct	Follow club agenda outline Choose format for holiday	**Looking at Basics:** Long-term debt to capitalization	Selected Members do research for next meeting.

MONTH	CLUB BUSINESS	EDUCATION	HOMEWORK / OTHER
	party (potluck, catered, dining out, etc.) Choose day/time for club holiday party	Institutional ownership	
Nov	Follow club agenda outline Finalize assignments/costs for holiday party	Stock splits: what do they mean?	Remind Members about holiday party preparations and confirm each Member's contribution.
Dec	Holiday party!		Selected Members do research for next meeting.

About the Authors

Chris Kiklas is an author, coach, speaker, leader and technology executive who loves to transform groups and communities. Chris is passionate about helping people create new ideas and bring them to life. When not working on projects, he enjoys spending time with his dog, Clarise, and traveling the world, meeting new people and experiencing new cultures.

Jan Mitchell Johnson is a grant writer and consultant to the education super stars and has won almost $250 million for her clients. She recently moved from Houston back to her home town of Panama City, Florida where (in her *spare* time) she sells real estate and manages three vacation properties, which she rents on Airbnb. She's exhausted a lot, it's true, but her reward for all those long nights at the computer is downtime on a beautiful beach and trips to Shell Island on her jet ski.

Jason Smith is an engineer, coach, and consultant who loves to solve problems. Jason is passionate about freedom; freedom in life, freedom in business, freedom in yourself. Much of what drives him is his desire to impart some sense of freedom and confidence in others. In his free time, Jason enjoys spending time with his wife, Carla, his son, Nicholas, and watching sports (Steelers, Texans, Dynamo, Astros).

WOWZA!
You've FINISHED the book!

If you whizzed past our previous request for a review (because you were so enthralled and didn't want to stop reading even for one minute—and who could blame you?), here's your second chance!

Please review our book on Amazon (amazon.com) and let us (and other readers) know what you got from the time you INVESTED with us. We'd be honored to read your feedback, and you may even end up in lights on our Rich on Fifty web site!

If you're on **Team Goodreads** (goodreads.com), you can leave your review on that book lovers' site.

And if you're an over-achiever, you can do BOTH!

Thanks for reading all the way to the very end. Now go out, get your friends together, and all of you, GET RICH ON FIFTY!

Made in the USA
Lexington, KY
28 January 2019